UX Writing Essentials: a simple guide for all

by Atila Velo

Table of Contents

About the author

Atila Velo is from the Y generation, the last generation of the 20th century. His first experience with the internet was of pages made with tables, where the connection was dial-up and made a very distinct sound. That sound will never be forgotten because what followed was a universe of slow possibilities for acquiring knowledge, some types of entertainment, a variety of tools (including a lot of useless shareware), communication with people from around the world, and endless learning.

Always had a knack for remote controls, so he specialized in UX Design. Just kidding! He earned his Bachelor's degree in Advertising, followed by a post-graduation in Communication and Marketing. Next month, he will complete his second post-graduation in User Experience and User Interface. He has taken many courses, bootcamps, and events in the realm of user experience (UX). He started working with book and magazine layout, transitioned to advertising copywriting, delved into web writing, and finally, landed in this branch of design with UX Writing, Content Design, and leading Product Designers, including in DesignOps. In 2023, he also taught UX Writing in the MBA course in User Experience at Impacta College: 7 hours of original content, practical exercises with individualized feedback, and exams.

In 2022, he released his first book on UX Writing in Portuguese, and in 2023, he launched the sequel. Available for reading through

Kindle Unlimited, they have already surpassed 30,000 pages read together!

Keeping this audience in mind, Atila decided to expand to people who do not understand the Portuguese language, opting for English, which has long been the most globalized language. You are reading the result of this effort right now. "UX Writing Essentials: a simple guide for all" is his first book in English.

He is married, vegetarian, and has five cats that he considers as his children. Loves rock'n'roll and coffee.

Introduction

Design is so much more than we are used to thinking! Even after working as a graphic designer for magazines and books, and then transitioning to copywriting—engaging with both digital and print ads—I discovered that I hadn't fully grasped the immense depth and breadth of design.

Undoubtedly, those known as UX Writers are, in fact, Content Designers. To be a proficient UX Writer, one must explore the intricacies of design: its particularities, methodologies, frameworks, ceremonies, research techniques, and much more. A skilled UX Writer must comprehend the language of a UX Designer (or Product Designer) and understand the rationale behind a chosen path over another. While this book encapsulates the essentials needed to comprehend UX Writing, becoming an exceptional UX Writer involves delving deeper into design, even if only in theory.

Here, you'll discover shared elements between writers and designers—quite a lot, I can assure you. This book aims to provide the essential aspects, combining content from my two UX Writing books published in Portuguese. It ensures that the basics are covered for beginners, the curious, and those contemplating a career shift. Additionally, it offers supplementary knowledge for those already working as UX Writers. If you are a senior or a specialist professional, you may not find entirely new information here. Nevertheless, it serves as a good memory refresher, as we don't use all our knowledge all the time, and some details might be forgotten.

I endeavored to write in a fresh, accessible, and easy-to-read manner so that everyone can enjoy the book and keep it within reach for quick reference. The process left me tired, but the satisfaction of taking my content to a global audience is immeasurable. Whether read by a single individual or becoming a best-seller, my objective is to share, and every person matters.

I hope you enjoy this book, have fun, and find success in your career!

Atila Velo

For what and for whom is this book?

With this book, I aim to make the essential knowledge about the work of UX Writers easy to access. I want it to be simple and clear so that anyone can understand the unique aspects, expertise, and theories of this profession.

The foundation of this material includes my practical knowledge, collective insights gathered from professionals worldwide who share their opinions and experiences online, along with theoretical knowledge drawn from books such as 'Strategic Writing for UX' by Torrey Podmajersky, 'Microcopy: The Complete Guide' by Kinneret Yifrah, 'Em busca de boas práticas de UX Writing' by Bruno Rodrigues, as well as other articles, blogs, LinkedIn posts, webinars, and conversations with seasoned professionals.

People from marketing, communication, and writing-related fields can use this book as their first introduction to UX Writing, whether out of curiosity or with the intention of transitioning careers.

Here, I discuss what we can consider the evolution of written text. After it, came radio and television, which "talked" to us. Similarly, the texts on current screens need to "talk" with people, "humanizing" technology.

It is a kind of anthropomorphism of interfaces, much like what has been happening more recently with generative artificial intelligences that "talk" with people — or at least that's the experience people feel like they're having.

However, it's important to emphasize right from the start that UX Writers need to study extensively about Design, its methodologies, theories, and frameworks, as well as information architecture, the details of interactive interfaces, user experience heuristics, research methods more associated with design than copywriting, in short, there is a vast and very specific universe when we think about user experience, even when focusing solely on writing.

Free yourself from ego: expertise adds value but can be pitfalls

One of the most respected names in Brazil when it comes to writing for the digital realm, from web writing to UX Writing, is the dear Bruno Rodrigues, who wrote the preface for my first book. He often uses a fantastic phrase that captures the attitude we, as writing professionals focusing on end-users, should adopt: "come in and hang your ego behind the door."

What does this mean? It indicates that, despite having practical experience, extensive theoretical knowledge, excellent common sense, sharp intuition, and many beliefs about who our audience is and how they function, we cannot rely on any of that to make crucial decisions in UX Writing.

We need to research, analyze, study, document, and continue learning daily about the users of our products. As new features are added to products, the profile of users may also change, either due to a natural evolution in people's proficiency with digital interfaces or simply because there has been a renewal in our customer base.

This means we cannot get accustomed to one profile and believe that we know everything there is to know about those people. This is another critique we can make of the use of personas, which, if not constantly updated, may cease to represent the audience reliably.

Therefore, just as in Eastern philosophical traditions, free yourself from your ego and associated dogmas. Embrace the curiosity of a child, practice empathy, and never stop studying.

What is User Experience?

User Experience (UX) has been a concern for strategic brands for a long time. The term UX, originating from the English phrase "user experience," dates back to the 1990s. However, it was in the last two decades that this term gained strength and relevance. Therefore, from the need to provide increasingly better, more personalized, and consistent experiences, the optimization of User Experience emerged.

Initially, all attention was focused on visual design: how design could be more fluid, responsive, integrated, dynamic; how design could communicate with the user, guide them, be more humanized, and less robotic. UX Designers, specialists in this type of creation, and UX Researchers, sometimes a role also played by UX Designers, emerged. To achieve the best results, many research, testing, and interview sessions are conducted by these professionals. And the process is usually continuous: User Experience professionals revisit and resume their work to refine it, conduct new tests, and discover how to further increase the efficiency of the design.

However, the interfaces of digital products and, more broadly, the touchpoints between the customer and the brand, moments we can consider as part of the User Experience, are not made up only of graphic elements. Texts (or microcopy) are also necessary, often indispensable, to engage and instruct customers. Hence, the specialization of writing for User Experience emerged — UX Writing. There is some controversy about the scope of the UX Writer's work and what is beyond it. Still, personally, I believe that we could operate beyond interactions in digital interfaces and microcopy.

The differentiation between Customer Experience (CX) and User Experience (UX) is that the former encompasses the entire customer journey and it's more focused on customer service and problem resolution, while the latter works only with specific digital products in which the customer plays the role of a user. An end-to-end view of a person's experience with a particular brand would be the work of service designers, in case you are interested in that role. But there is consistently low demand for this professional profile, as companies have not fully embraced service designers as an essential role within product design teams. As a result, the tasks they perform tend to be distributed among other user experience roles.

To determine the course of User Experience work, some questions need to be addressed, such as: What is the product? When will the user use it? Why should the user use it? How will the user use it? Where will this product be useful to the user? Lastly, who is this user?

So, we move on to the discovery stage, a traditional step in the double diamond design process, using various research techniques and data creation to, for example, develop multiple personas to illustrate different user types more vividly than with just demographic data. Of course, this requires qualitative research, such as interviews, to understand the individuals. After all, everything in user experience revolves around people: the success of those using our products and, in turn, generating profit for the company.

What are microtexts?

Microtext, microcopy, or even UX copy are different ways of referring to the type of writing (originating from advertising or copywriting) that consists of few characters, few lines, texts that require maximum conciseness, and, in some cases, a lot of personality. Striking the balance between the diminutive size of the text and the personality it can convey is part of the challenging mission of the UX Writer.

The book "Microcopy: The Complete Guide" by Kinneret Yifrah has become the primary reference on the topic of microcopy. However, the term wasn't popularized by its author.

Long before the book, in 2009, a guy named Joshua Porter wrote a post titled "Writing Microcopy." In it, Porter shared how he had solved a significant problem with a small piece of text: in the e-commerce where he worked, 5% to 10% of purchases were failing due to an error in the billing address.

What was his insight? He added a simple message below the address field, instructing the user that it should be the same as the credit card billing address. Errors stopped, and the e-commerce became more successful. At the time, the post resonated well, and many people thanked Joshua Porter for giving a name to the practice of writing small texts for digital products.

In her book, Kinneret Yifrah defines microtext as the words or phrases in the interface directly related to the actions the user performs:

- Motivation before the action;

- Instructions accompanying the action;
- and the response (feedback) after the user has completed the action.

We'll see some examples later on. For now, just understand that the vast majority of microtexts are part of apps or websites and generate some type of interaction in these digital interfaces.

What else is UX Writing?

UX Writing instructs people in a more holistic and comprehensive manner. It's related to Copywriting (traditional advertising writing) and Webwriting (writing for the internet), and it considers the entire User Experience while informing, instructing, guiding, clarifying, and engaging — always in line with the brand or product's tone of voice.

In summary, UX Writing is about writing, revising, and optimizing texts with the support of research and testing. But how far does User Experience go? I believe that email subjects and push notifications (from apps or websites), for example, are within the scope of UX. What else? Well, internal signage in a company is often overlooked because it's not digital, but it could be a great application of the talents of a good UX Writer. Instead of generic and cold messages, wouldn't it be better to have texts consistent with the voice the brand adopts in its marketing and branding strategy? Another very important thing: UX Writers rely heavily on feedback and assistance from other professionals, such as UX designers (or Product Designers), UX researchers, developers, product managers, customer support team, among other stakeholders.

UX Writing is about a win-win: the text helps the user get what they want while helping the company get what it wants from the user.

Speaking of function, UX Writing serves to promote some action, facilitating and engaging the user on the website or app. It provides reassurance to the user when they are unsure whether to register and provide their personal data. It also guides the user to the next steps, the next stages that the product has to offer (until reaching the company's goal). UX Writing removes ambiguities by ensuring clarity and transparency of information, and it helps the user calm down when there is a system error or uncertainties in their mind.

In practice, the UX Writer is someone who designs content to create seamless experiences. That's why in some companies, UX Writers are called Content Designers.

The types of teams in which a UX Writer works

Generally, one of three more common models is adopted: squad-based work, work that spans different squads (cross), or consultancy.

When it's possible to exclusively dedicate oneself to a single squad, the UX Writer has the opportunity to participate in all ceremonies and follow the development of products and features from start to finish. They can be involved in all stages of the double diamond (we'll talk more about it later) and may have more time for research and testing.

The form that, in my experience, seems to be the most common is that of a single UX Writer serving multiple squads, in a model that spans teams, also called cross-squads. In this format, workload management can become challenging, especially if the team consists of only one person (a phenomenon popularly known as "solo team").

It's necessary to coordinate with the team and stakeholders on how ceremonies will be prioritized because it's impossible to participate in all the key ones happening in every squad. In this model, the UX Writer needs to rely heavily on the partnership of Product Designers and sometimes Product Managers to gain sufficient context for UX Writing work to be done in the best way. This includes the production of proto-copies (or low-fidelity microtexts) by Product Designers.

It's strategic for these professionals to have some good understanding of writing for the user experience so that they can create a first version. Thus, even if it's outside the brand's tone and voice and contains some spelling errors, the person truly specialized in writing will find, in the prototypes, a first version sufficient for understanding the flow being designed, focusing more on refinement.

In consultancies or specialized agencies, UX Writing professionals may work with one or more products and features simultaneously, with the volume of work and their involvement in each initiative varying greatly. It's the model that provides the greatest variety of products, segments, and contexts, but it can be very challenging to work with tight deadlines to immerse and discover the product's users, as well as the peculiarities of each brand's voice.

We need to talk about prioritization

Building on the three types of projects, let's address the issue of prioritizing tasks. When working in a single squad, it might be feasible to tackle tasks in the chronological order they arise. However, when serving more than one squad or working on multiple projects simultaneously, it's necessary to establish criteria to ensure that the overall quality of your deliveries doesn't decline, and it remains humanly possible to complete everything.

In my case, working across multiple squads, I chose to prioritize based on what was most crucial for the business: the perception of end customers. So, I actively participated in the product ceremonies that had more direct interaction with end customers, seeking deep involvement throughout the entire process.

As for the other products, given my limited attention, I heavily relied on the assistance of dedicated Product Designers from the squads to provide context on what we were aiming for with each project, especially those involving internal company clients.

Important meetings for the UX writer

As discussed in the previous chapter, prioritization is essential for maintaining the quality of the UX writer's deliverables. Therefore, choosing the meetings and ceremonies to attend is a crucial process for such professionals, as it will determine their focus areas, where they will invest most of their time, and also contribute to maintaining their mental well-being.

Typically, when companies work with the Design + Product + Technology triad, they adopt agile methodologies. In this scenario, we can mention some ceremonies that may be more important for gaining context, participating in discovery and research stages, and supporting overall ideation, not just the text. The UX Writer community in Brazil loves to repeat: **it's not just a little text!**

So, the suggestion is to participate, when possible, in discovery, planning, review, some refinement, and retrospective meetings. Daily stand-ups usually serve to report on the progress of work, so they might be a waste of time for UX Writers.

Join them only if you have any questions and want to discuss them with the entire squad or if someone invites you specifically. But if you're serving multiple squads, imagine how it would be possible for you to attend all the daily rituals?

Voice and tone of a brand: what are those things?

Every professional working with marketing communication texts (a.k.a. Copywriter) needs to embody the personality of the brand they are working with so that their texts feel authentic, unique, and true to that brand. Part of this personality is what defines the voice of a brand. This is because, even though we know that text on a screen is not a human being talking, people respond to computers and many electronic devices as if they were human. Therefore, when devices malfunction, people feel anger, curse, and even physically harm the poor devices. We are egocentric beings who see faces where they don't exist (smileys being a great example), and we attribute personalities to the most diverse things, including brands.

For example, it's easy to say that Apple is sophisticated, H&M is democratic, Harley Davidson is rebellious, and Target is approachable. These are established examples, so when we see an ad or use a website or app from these brands, we expect them to have a voice that corresponds to the adjectives we associate with them. The tone of the voice will vary depending on the context, but we also expect Apple to have a more serious (but not stern) and calm tone, while Harley Davidson is more youthful and noisy.

It's the UX Writer's responsibility to discover the voice and tones of each brand they work with. This discovery occurs through extensive research on the company's origin, principles, values, and existing communications, as well as through conversations with stakeholders. They should create a scale with opposing characteristics and determine where the brand falls on it: is it more serious or playful? More direct or conversational? More formal or informal? What is its speaking pace? Does it use foreign terms or regional phrases? And slang? Swear words? Emojis? Memes? Creating brand personas can help arrive at the voice and its tones.

And, obviously, reaching a brand voice can (or should) be a collaborative task in perfect harmony with teams from marketing, branding, customer satisfaction, sales, after-sales, as well as key stakeholders and C-level executives.

What is a brand persona?

A successful brand maintains consistency in its communication, meaning it is recognizable and speaks in a way the customer expects. Imagine if, suddenly, Ferrari started trying to sell its cars based on fuel economy and ease of maintenance? Or if Best Buy aired minimalist ads without visible prices, without animated narration, and all sophisticated? It would be, at the very least, strange, wouldn't it?

This is because the brand persona (the person we project onto the brand) is not compatible with that specific profile.

If it were a person, what would Ferrari be like? Athletic and wealthy, for example. And Best Buy? It would be a more simple and humble person.

This exercise of imagining human characteristics behind a brand leads us to the creation of brand personas — a variation of buyer personas, widely used in communication and marketing strategies.

When a brand is created, it usually has some declared purposes — and in its day-to-day, other personality traits can be identified. The old trio of vision, mission, and values often guides this personality. If this doesn't happen, there is a dissonance between what the brand claims to be and what it is — which can be a formula for failure. But it's not only in the creation of the brand that we can evaluate the voice and tone: when launching a new product, website, or application, it's also a good opportunity to discover the attributes that stand out in that brand; and, of course, when the company decides to invest in UX Writing.

But you don't need to literally create a brand persona; you just need part of the methodology to identify the most striking characteristics, the values evoked, and the sensations caused by the brand.

Talking to users (customers) of the brands is essential to discover which adjectives are most attributed, most associated with that brand.

How to define the voice (and its tones) of a brand?

For weeks, the UX Writing professional must conduct the necessary analysis to obtain the voice (and its tones) of a brand. It should be documentation that precisely defines the brand's personality and how it translates into the way the brand communicates, especially in texts. This document will be useful not only for UX Writers but also for all other writing professionals, such as copywriters, web writers, social media, CX professionals, CRM, among others.

Torrey Podmajersky suggests a table that cross-references the top three product principles with the following characteristics: **concepts** (what these principles mean); **vocabulary** (words associated with the principles); **verbosity** (how much the brand will speak according to the principles); **grammar** (what type of writing and rules will be adopted or not according to the principles); **punctuation** (the amount of commas, exclamation use, among other punctuation peculiarities related to the principles); and, finally, **capitalization** (whether these principles imply using uppercase letters, when and where).

The work should begin with a thorough examination of all the brand's previous materials, especially style guides and visual identity guides. Then, listen to what the target audience says about the brand and its segment. From there, assemble a more appropriate vocabulary for the brand. It is relevant to interview users/customers and also important people in the company, asking about the brand and its audience. Documenting all the information you find, you will arrive at raw material that, when refined, will give rise to the voice (and its tones) of the brand.

It will be a guide on how the brand should communicate. It should list some core values, describe them, and provide examples. It should also indicate other nuances of the voice, give examples of different situations, and how the tone of voice should be. The Nielsen Norman Group suggests working on four dimensions: **fun** or **serious**, **formal** or **casual**, **ceremonious** or **irreverent**, **enthusiastic** or **direct**. I also like Cris Luckner's suggestion to add one more dimension: **popular** or **refined**. Defining the brand's tone of voice within these dimensions allows you to select the most appropriate tone of voice for each situation.

We must also define the target audience for each brand and its main characteristics: this mapping will guide the construction of controlled vocabulary (or reference vocabulary), a source to consult which words should prevail in communication. Finally, determine what relationship the brand has with its audience: is it friendly? Is it maternal? Is it a business partner? Is it a teacher? Knowing the type of relationship the brand has with its audience will make it much easier to plan and develop efficient and dialogical (or conversational) content.

Finally, we can also use other resources to further define "who the brand is," such as mood boards, defining the brand's music, which fictional character the brand is, if the brand were a car, what would it be? Among other variations. There is also a brand positioning within some predefined options, known as the 12 archetypes of brands — a methodology based on the work of Carl Gustav Jung.

Examples of publicly available guides:

- MailChimp (https://styleguide.mailchimp.com/),
- Conscious (https://consciousstyleguide.com/),

- Shopify (https://polaris.shopify.com/content/product-content),
- Intuit (https://contentdesign.intuit.com/),
- Monzo (https://monzo.com/tone-of-voice/),
- Microsoft (https://docs.microsoft.com/en-us/style-guide/welcome/),
- Canada Post Corporation (https://www.canadapost.ca/cpc/en/designsystem/mercury/ux-writing.page)
- UK Government (https://www.gov.uk/government/content-publishing).

Proximity to Branding, Marketing, Advertising, and Growth

You probably already know, but it doesn't hurt to remind: branding is something that emerged a long time ago, in a rudimentary form, when ranchers began to brand their cattle and small producers started putting their names, fingerprints, or drawings that set their products apart from others. Businesses also began using writing on walls or posters to indicate product availability, all of this in the early civilizations of human history, in the region that is now Iraq, ancient Mesopotamia.

Marketing, which is the study of market demands and products or services that can satisfy them, has evolved, and almost sixty years ago, a man named Philip Kotler was already recording best practices in the profession. The role of individuals specializing in marketing, branding, advertising, media, and growth is directly related to the experiences a company offers its customers. Therefore, there are many points of contact or intersection between the work of User Experience and these areas.

Ideally, the tone and voice guide created by UX Writers should be consistent with the brand manual, and there should be a deep alignment of discourse and brand persona among design teams, marketing, branding, etc.

For example, notifications sent by the application to people's smartphones (push notifications), when transactional — meaning they inform users about an update in their journey — can be crafted in partnership with UX Writers. On the other hand, promotional content aimed at generating a sale, converting a lead, or other objectives more related to marketing strategies can be handled by the respective team — provided they speak the same language, meaning they use the same brand voice.

The same applies to emails and their sequences — and all other types of communication, from customer service to public relations, advertising campaigns, and giveaways.

Sharing with other departments

Design (both digital and graphic), branding, growth, marketing, customer relationship management (CRM), customer experience (CX), internal communication, social media, advertisements, email sequences (and also SMS or WhatsApp) that inform process stages, and other materials (that I probably forgot right now) are all interconnected, united by the company's goal of creating the best possible experience with the brand and its products and/or services. So, there are many areas that overlap in terms of responsibilities, governance, and decision-making power.

The design team needs maturity to build strong relationships with other departments because everyone must collaborate to ensure that any experience with the brand is consistent, that no channel deviates, seems like another brand persona, or offers inferior quality.

For example, the tone and voice guide need to be 100% aligned with all other departments that "speak" on behalf of the company. Everyone that establishes a communication with a customer (or a user) has to follow the voice of the brand and the tones indicated within the guide, otherwise the experience may seem fragmented to the person on the other side, also known as the customer or the user.

What is conversational content?

As we discussed earlier, humans tend to treat machines (computers, tablets, smartphones, and even household appliances) as if they were people. Since 2022, treating artificial intelligences as people has become commonplace, with individuals perceiving reactive systems as conscious beings.

There's even an article from the Nielsen Norman Group that addresses the 4 degrees of AI anthropomorphism: **1. Courtesy** - the user is polite and friendly; **2. Reinforcement** - the user praises the AI as feedback; **3. Roleplay** - the person imagines or asks the AI to interpret a role so they can interact; and **4. Companionship** - when people become attached (or addicted?) to the AIs as if they were friends or family. This is a direct consequence of the growing isolation of younger generations, who have a difficult time interacting live, in person, cannot engage in small talk, or break the ice.

Due to this behavior and perception, the best experiences are achieved when the user feels like they are having a dialogue or conversation with an application, website, or any other interface. We should, therefore, aim to create dialogues, not just simple texts. The interface "speaks," and the user "responds." For example:

A product's landing page can engage in a conversation with the visitor and, in the end, offer a button that says "I want it." By clicking the button, the user is, in a way, responding to the proposal, the question posed by the landing page.

But it's not just that. One must always imagine how a brand representative would act in the specific situations for which the UX Writer will write. Would they say "good morning" in a more formal manner or greet with a simple "hello"? When giving instructions, would the representative speak in a more categorical or commanding tone, using imperative verbs, or would they be more delicate and use infinitive verbs? "Use the app now: open the app and click the Start button" or "To use the app, just open it and click the Start button"? There's no right or wrong; there's only what is compatible with your brand's voice and what is not.

It's up to the UX Writer (in harmony with marketing, branding, etc.) to decide and document how such dialogues between the brand and users should be. As a general rule, it's better to write in a way that is closer to how we speak rather than how we write. Seriously, it can be very different from one to the other! But be careful not to compromise the text's understanding: always read, reread, read aloud, submit to another professional, or even have a friend read it to see if they understand what you mean — ensure that, with those words, the message is being successfully conveyed.

In an ideal scenario, users are recruited to read the texts in interfaces, and thus, the UX team can verify what works best for that audience. We will approach UX Writing tests later.

Why do personas matter?

Personas are fictional representations that exemplify the profile of product users. More specific and detailed than the target audience, they provide more information to create a profile, sometimes stereotyped, of potential users. Knowing the audience is essential to develop empathy and understand exactly how we should communicate with them, which is why (buyer) personas are so important. There are various tutorials on how to create personas on the internet, so I won't delve into the subject here — especially because, quite often, when the UX Writer thinks about creating buyer personas, they discover that someone from Marketing, for example, has already created them.

It's worth mentioning that when we build personas only with quantitative and demographic data, they don't truly become personas; we call them protopersonas. Only after careful qualitative research do personas become complete and come closer to truly representing users.

I've heard many people say they don't believe in personas for the user experience field. Well, they should represent the customers of a particular brand, essentially an idealized person with characteristics most likely found in their audience. But often, personas are interesting research deliverables that are never actually used.

They could help the entire company base its efforts, always keeping that profile in mind, including the design team, to avoid personal biases and beliefs about the needs of users. However, it's common for companies to create one or two personas and never think about them again. It's also very likely that they were created based on incorrect data and, therefore, don't solve anything.

The ideal scenario is that generating personas is a collaborative effort involving all areas of the company that can benefit from a well-defined profile, along with a full understanding of the rigor in collecting the data that inspires the creation of such profiles. Another important thing to remember is that there won't be one absolute, definitive persona that is perfect for all areas and scenarios analyzed. Each created persona should have a final goal related to the company's business.

For example, a large shoe manufacturer might need a persona for women's sneakers, another for men's sneakers, another for unisex flip-flops, and so on. If the UX team is creating a persona, they can define that it's the persona that will benefit the most from the feature they are studying in the discovery phase. They will always be different people because every audience is heterogeneous to some degree, no matter the company.

Ironically, the characteristic that most sets personas apart from impersonal generalizations, the fact that they have a unique and exclusive personality, is what generates the most controversy and misunderstanding. When in doubt, my suggestion is simple: test it. Create a persona (or a simpler protopersona) with a specific goal in mind and see if it helps with planning and ideation. Who knows?

Recommended reading to help you with personas: Persona Scope: Why Most UX Research Is Misguided (https://www.nngroup.com/articles/persona-scope/).

Why do user journeys matter?

Speaking of the user's journey, it should be mapped from the first contact the person has with the brand to post-sales actions. This mapping will identify all opportunities to delight the user, resolve or anticipate problems, with rich details about how the user feels at each stage, allowing reflection on how we can improve them. Basically, the map consists of at least four rows and as many columns as necessary. The essential rows are: touchpoints, user actions, user needs, and how the user feels. The columns describe the experience, step by step.

Understanding the user journey is crucial for creating a seamless and positive experience. It starts with the initial interaction a person has with a brand and extends through all subsequent stages, including post-sales. By mapping this journey, we can pinpoint various touchpoints, user actions, and needs, as well as the emotional responses users may have at each step. This detailed overview allows for a comprehensive understanding of the user experience, revealing areas for improvement and enhancement.

The concept of touchpoints is essential in user journey mapping. These are the specific points of interaction between the user and the brand, whether it's a website visit, an email exchange, or a customer service call. Identifying and analyzing these touchpoints provide valuable insights into how users engage with the brand, helping to tailor experiences that meet their expectations and needs. A positive touchpoint can significantly impact the overall perception of the brand.

User actions, another key component of the journey map, outline the steps users take in their interactions with the brand. This includes actions such as browsing products, making a purchase, or seeking customer support. Understanding these actions is fundamental to anticipating user needs and ensuring a smooth and intuitive experience. By aligning the user's actions with their expectations, brands can create more effective and user-friendly interfaces that contribute to overall satisfaction.

Additionally, delving into user needs and emotions at each stage of the journey provides deeper insights. This analysis helps in designing experiences that not only fulfill functional requirements but also resonate with users on an emotional level. By acknowledging and addressing user needs and emotions, brands can foster a stronger connection, leading to increased loyalty and positive word-of-mouth. In essence, user journey mapping is a powerful tool for refining the user experience, enhancing satisfaction, and building lasting relationships with customers.

Other crucial elements that may be part of a user journey include identifying pain points and areas of improvement, understanding the gains or benefits users seek, and considering various factors. By comprehensively mapping these aspects, brands can refine their strategies to address user needs, provide solutions, and continually enhance the overall user experience, ensuring that users not only overcome challenges but also achieve their desired gains.

How does UX Writing tell stories?

From the moment the user discovers the brand to when they cease to be a user, an entire story unfolds. It begins back in the first instance when the prospect was impacted by any communication from the brand, paid or unpaid. It traverses the stages of converting the prospect into a lead, nurturing the lead for qualification, transforming them into a customer, and ensuring their satisfaction post-contact with the brand, in after-sales and support.

Therefore, it is crucial to employ at least four elements derived from storytelling techniques — the famous narrative arc — to inspire us whenever it is necessary to develop stories that we will convey to our users:

1. Connecting with the audience:

To connect with the audience, it is essential to speak directly to them. Use a more friendly and approachable language and make it clear that the product is there to serve the user.

2. Creating the villain/problem:

Knowing that the user needs the product to solve a problem, in this stage, we must emphasize that the product is there to defeat the villain of the story, meaning to solve the user's problem.

3. Definitive solution:

The product needs to sell itself, convincing the user that it is the ideal solution to their initial problem. Once converted and satisfied, the user starts trusting the product.

4. Moral of the story:

In the end, the user returns to their comfort zone, but with the villain defeated (problem solved) and great satisfaction in having achieved the goal that the product helped them accomplish.

For instance, let's look at the Hemingway app (https://hemingwayapp.com/), a very useful tool for checking the readability level of a text. So, when we write, we encounter the problem: is the text easy to understand? Knowing the tool, either through research or recommendation, we immediately connect with it because it seems easy to use. The homepage is already the application's interface, very inviting and intuitive.

We have the problem and the connection with the audience; now, the definitive solution is missing: just copy and paste your text into the application for it to provide you with a score (the lower, the better). Keeping that in mind, we can make the necessary adjustments (sometimes even recommended by the tool) and "return home" with a sense of accomplishment, that is, with the moral of the story that the application was genuinely helpful and helped us solve the problem.

Another example: DoorDash or Uber Eats brands connect with the audience through widely promoted ads and promotions. We have a clearly defined villain: hunger. Those apps connect the user to hundreds of restaurant options, thus being the definitive solution. The moral of the story is that people end up satisfied with the experience and return to using the application.

Simple language: good for people, good for business

Plain Language, also known as Simple Language, is a technique of written communication that aims to make information more accessible and understandable for everyone, especially for people with disabilities or reading difficulties. This approach seeks to simplify writing, structure, design, and evaluation of texts, making them easier to understand for all individuals.

It is applicable in various situations, such as government texts, public services, legal documents, instruction manuals, among others. Through this approach, the goal is to eliminate the use of jargon, complex technical terms, and complicated language structures, replacing them with clear, concise, and objective language.

The use of Plain Language promotes inclusion by enabling access to information for people with different levels of reading and comprehension abilities. By adopting this technique, communicators (including UX Writers) make their content more accessible, contributing to the participation and empowerment of individuals, as well as promoting equal opportunities. Plain Language is a powerful tool to ensure the inclusion of everyone in society, reducing barriers and fostering citizenship.

It's important to remember that people with reading difficulties and disabilities represent a significant portion of the market. Let's look at the numbers: Overall, there are about 42.5 million Americans with disabilities, making up 13% of the civilian noninstitutionalized population, according to U.S. Census Bureau data from 2021. This group includes people with hearing, vision, cognitive, walking, self-care or independent living difficulties. Besides them, 15% of the total population have low literacy skills according to the governmental National Center for Education Statistics.

What are the most common texts in the UX Writer's routine?

Titles, buttons, links, registration or sign-up forms, password recovery, newsletter subscription, contact forms, error messages, confirmation messages, empty states, placeholders, labels, controls, error pages (including 404), search pages, and transition texts.

Titles

They should explain the context of that screen/page and what action should take place. Users often "scan" screens, reading titles and skipping more descriptive texts altogether. Therefore, the title should be comprehensive: always include a noun and a verb indicating possible actions in that situation, at that stage of the journey. "Do X thing" would be a generic formula, but you can be more creative than that (and test different versions to choose the best-performing one).

Clear and good enough title

The next image displays the homepage title of Clay Agency. It provides a clear statement about what the company is, where it operates, and its specializations:

Fun, but lacking the correct hierarchy of titles

Now, this next image shows the homepage of Best Lawyers. They unnecessarily repeat the brand's name as a primary title (it's already up there, as the logo), which can be considered a missed opportunity to start delivering another message to the public. However, their following title is clear enough and still plays with the 'case closed' expression in the end, a recognizable phrase used in courts, instead of using something like 'for sure,' 'definitely,' or 'period.'

Links

Simple links, distinct from buttons, should always serve as a tertiary function, following the primary and secondary actions that the company wants the user to take. For instance, on a login screen, we might have the 'Log In' button as the primary action, a secondary action, and below them, the 'Forgot your password?' link. There are also secondary buttons, which have less prominence than primary buttons and usually offer actions that are not the main focus of the screen where they appear or are not strategic for the business.

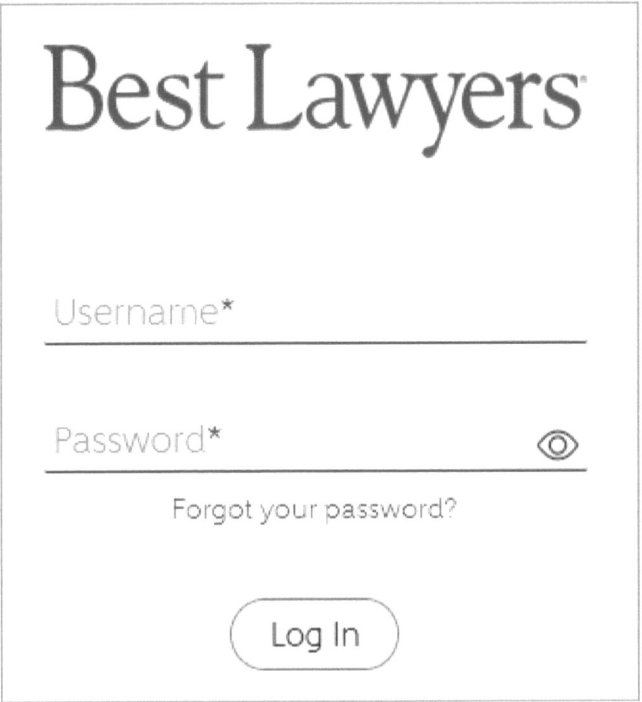

Registration Forms

First and foremost, it's essential to contemplate the significance of a registration form: it marks the beginning of a relationship between the brand and the user. Therefore, just like in any relationship's early stages, effort and attention to detail are crucial to convey credibility and encourage the user to provide their information.

Few people have the time and inclination to fill out lengthy forms, provide personal details, and create a new password. Hence, the microcopy surrounding a registration process plays a crucial role in assisting, motivating, and engaging the user — always in a friendly tone, as if having a conversation.

The Structure of a Registration Page

Considering the structure of an account creation or registration page, it should include:

- A friendly title
- An introductory text listing up to 3 advantages
- Fields for user data
- The button to submit the information

It's likely a good idea to include a notice about privacy policies and information security with an opt-in.

The following example, from the Neil Patel website tool called Ubersuggest, wastes the opportunity to use a more convincing title and provide more reasons for the user to register:

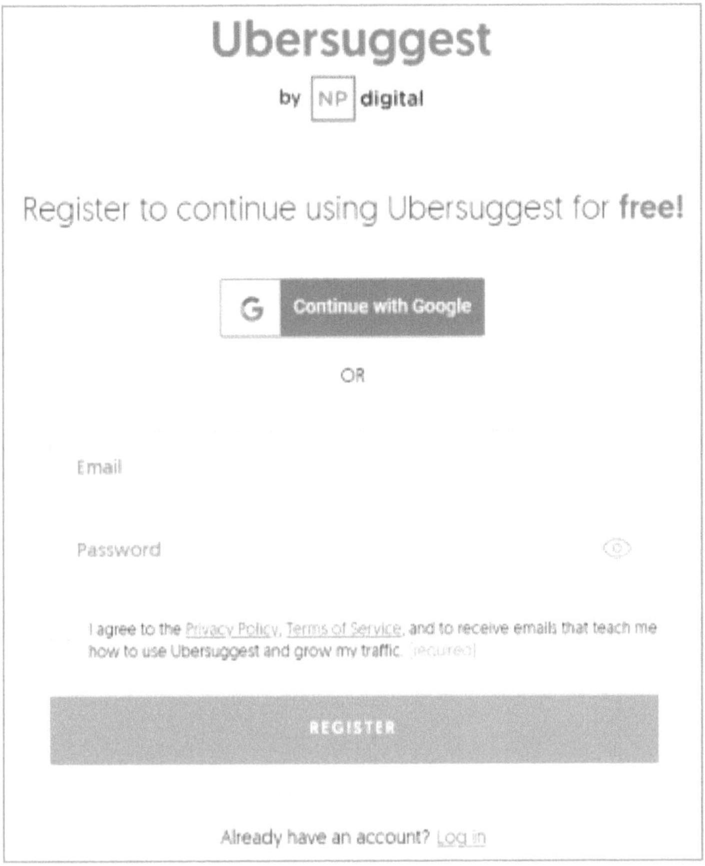
Ubersuggest
by NP digital
Register to continue using Ubersuggest for free!
G Continue with Google
OR
Email
Password
I agree to the Privacy Policy, Terms of Service, and to receive emails that teach me how to use Ubersuggest and grow my traffic.
REGISTER
Already have an account? Log in

The mail.com strategy is better because they reinforce the idea that the email is free in the title, then try to persuade the user by listing three arguments, with the above-average storage limit being a good reason to motivate the user to choose their services:

Create a free email account at mail.com
Quick and easy sign-up
Over 100 domain names
65 GB of free email storage
Check availability

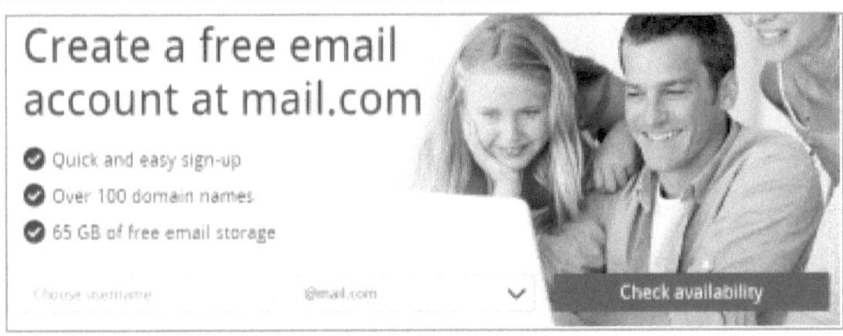

The Rockwell Automation create an account page doesn't state any benefit or give instructions, which is a wasted opportunity. However, their registration process features another important element in User Interface Design, focusing on providing the best User Experience: the steppers that indicate beforehand how many steps the user will have to go through to finish the account creation process. Telling the user where he or she is, what is possible to do on the current screen, and where we will take him or her after the activation of a button is a good practice, one of the 10 Nielsen Norman Group heuristics. Check how the screen lacks information about the benefits of an account and a guiding title but is transparent with the user by displaying what the next steps are:

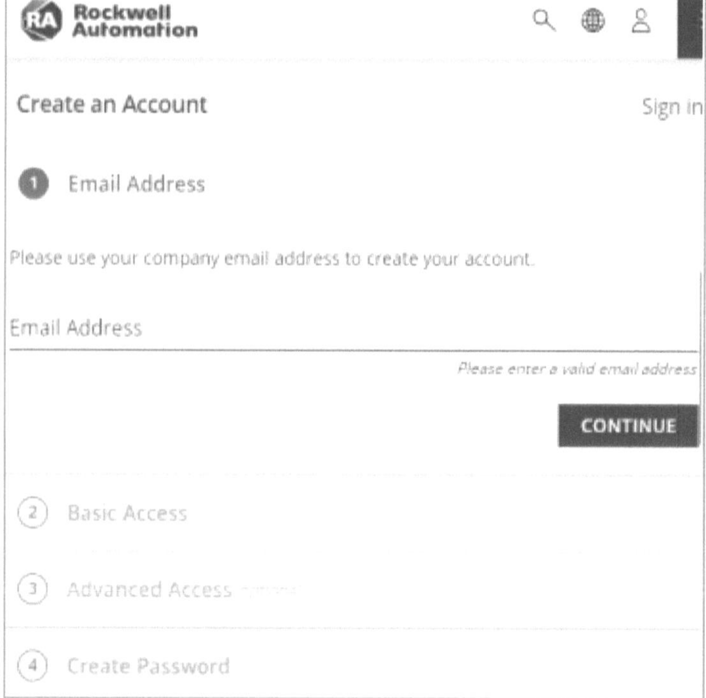

In the next form, the only positive aspect is the inclusion of steppers, indicating how many steps are left for the user to complete. However, the form lacks essential information, such as clarifying that it's specifically for a Playstation account and not a generic Sony account. The prioritization of information should focus on more relevant benefits, rather than emphasizing location and privacy:

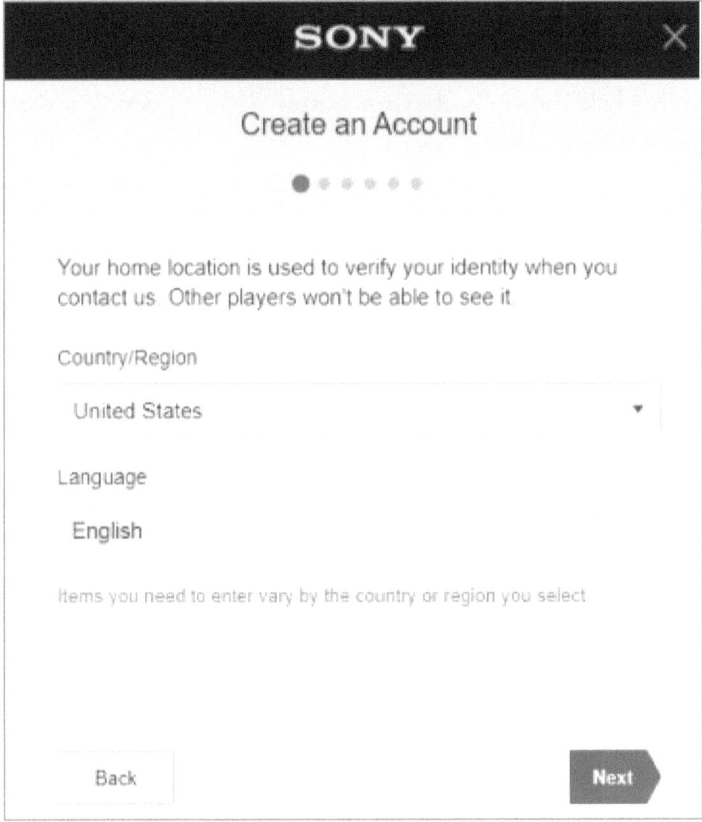

Password Recovery

When a user forgets their password, they're facing challenges and may be associating the brand with negative feelings. We want to avoid that! Therefore, it's crucial to take this demand seriously: use concise language, encourage the user to reset their password, and reaffirm that success is just around the corner.

The Riot Games form is minimalistic, requesting only the username. A dropdown menu follows, prompting the user to choose a location, defaulting to NA, explained only upon dropdown. NA refers to North America, and users can select other locations. The instructions are limited to "Enter your username," assuming users will intuitively click the right-chevron button (>), triggering a database request for the password recovery.

It's risky to use important buttons, like primary ones, without a label, text, or accompanying description. A simple 'Send' might be sufficient, but relying solely on a right arrow is risky because, as we always emphasize in UX, "you are not your user." Therefore, we can't assume that people will grasp the next step with just a symbol:

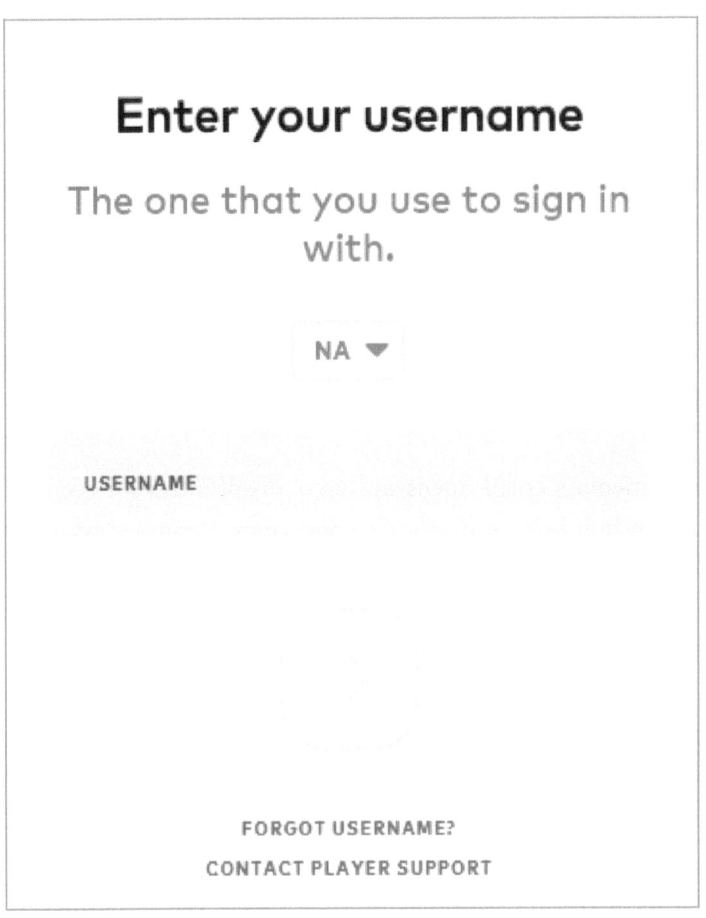

The World Health Organization's password recovery is simple, yet very straightforward and effective. The title is clear (although it could benefit from a first instruction or reinforcement), the description is good enough, and the button uses the obvious but adequate verb 'Submit.'

Newsletter Signup

Having someone's email opens up many possibilities for contact and relationship-building, and mature companies recognize the value of a good email base. Despite younger generations using email less or not at all, it remains a great business resource. However, it's crucial to convincingly communicate certain things to the user: that it will be beneficial for them, meaning they will enjoy the promised content, and also that you will handle their data carefully, including avoiding excessive emails (which would be considered spam).

Nike's newsletter form is minimalistic, prioritizing simplicity and clear content. While strategic in gathering additional details for targeted segments, the form may risk decreased user subscriptions due to extended information requests. Balancing data collection with user convenience remains crucial for optimal engagement.

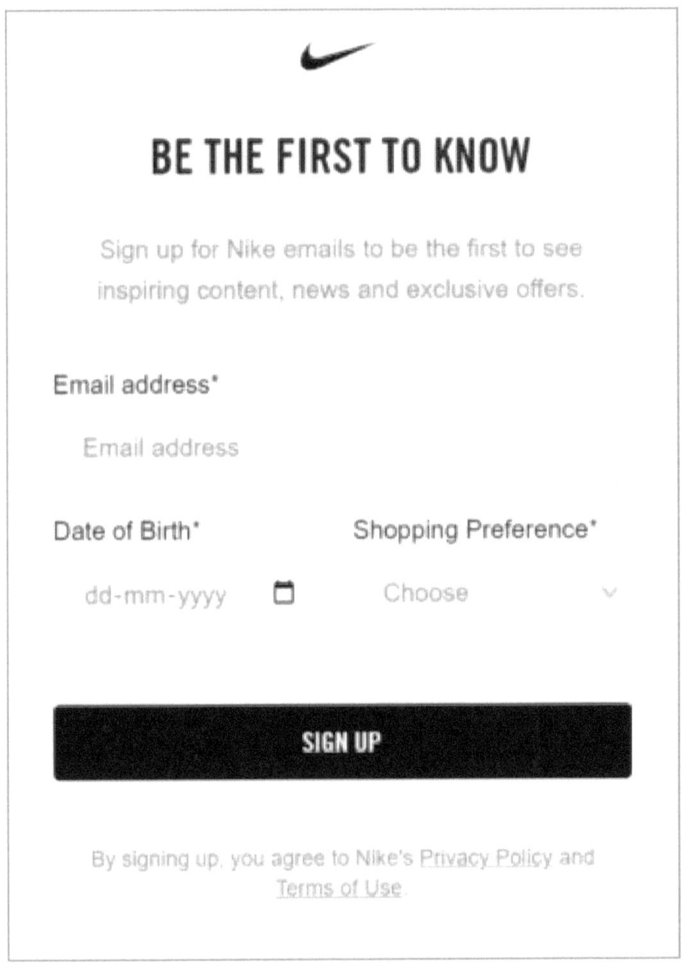

Brian Dean, an SEO expert, uses exclusivity on the descriptive title to attract newsletter subscribers. Highlighting exclusive SEO tips creates a desire to join, reinforced by a VP's testimony (social proof). The clean design and clear intent make it an excellent example:

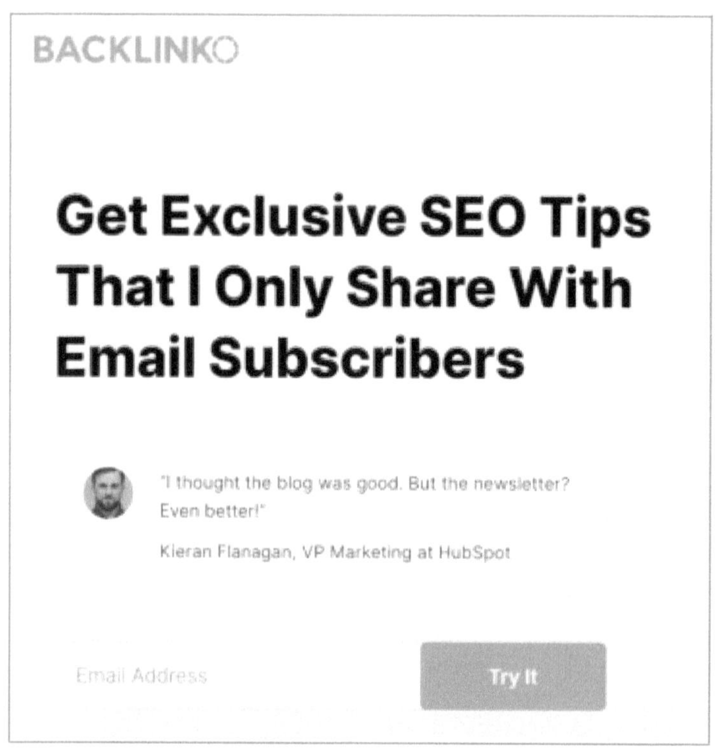

Contact Forms

Arguably one of the most crucial pages (or sections of the homepage) on a company's website, as it's the gateway to acquiring leads. However, this content often receives minimal attention. Many sites feature a mundane form under the title "Contact" or "Get in touch." Only that! Our goal is to encourage users to reach out (especially if they're potential leads), so we need to craft the text accordingly. Forget the clichés like "We'll be delighted to hear from you" or "Your feedback is important to us." Speak in the brand's voice, share the benefits, actively invite users to fill out the fields, and hit that submit button.

The following example presents an intriguing title, demonstrating that not all titles need to be imperative. It follows with a clear description, and the form fields are well-labeled with accompanying placeholders, exemplifying what users should input. The direct call-to-action button contributes to creating a highly effective contact form:

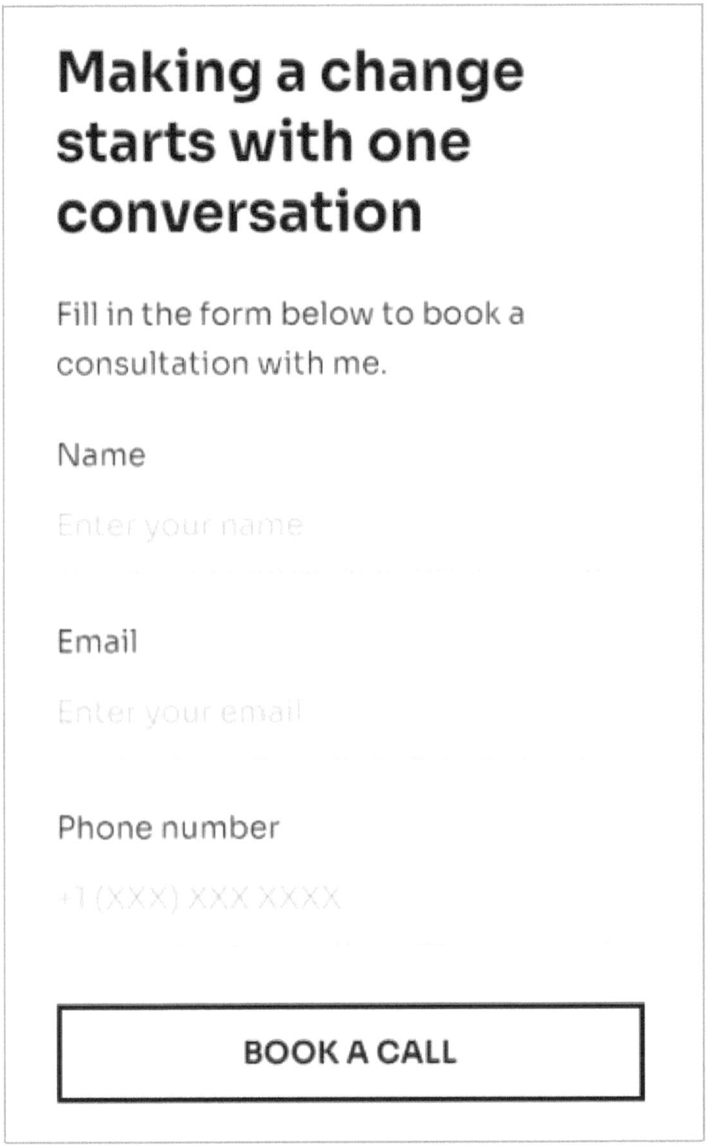

Making a change starts with one conversation

Fill in the form below to book a consultation with me.

Name

Enter your name

Email

Enter your email

Phone number

+1 (XXX) XXX XXXX

BOOK A CALL

Neil Patel's website provides another example. The clear title gets straight to the point, and the brief description outlines two reasons users might fill out the form. The form fields are easy to understand, with friendly and descriptive labels:

How can I help?

Do you have a question or are you interested in working with my team and me?
Just fill out the form fields below.

I'd like to chat about...

Name

Email Address

Message (remember, short & sweet please)

SUBMIT

Focus Lab takes a creative approach that might not align with most brands, but it resonates with their brand's voice and core values. Their form, designed like a story or a spoken statement, is refreshingly unique:

Fill this out so we can learn more about you and your needs.

My name is Full Name and I'm with Organization Name. I am in need of a partner to assist me with My Goals in a Snapshot, with a goal of having that completed on or near Date or Timeframe. I am looking to stay around a budget of -- . You can reach me at Email Address to get the conversation started. Thanks!

Send

About placeholders and labels

Labels are the words outside each form field, indicating what content should be inputted. Placeholders, conversely, are examples of what the user should type within the form fields. Some designers used to avoid labels and use only placeholders, which was terrible for usability since the instruction simply disappeared as the user selected that particular form field. Now, even together, combined, labels and placeholders, Nielsen Norman Group points out that placeholders are more damaging than helpful.

Avoid using placeholders as replacements for field labels for several reasons. First, disappearing placeholder text strains users' short-term memory, leading to frustration and potential errors. Users may forget hints, especially with complex or lengthy forms, and have to delete and revisit fields, disrupting their workflow. Without labels, users can't check their work or easily fix errors, making the form less user-friendly.

Additionally, the absence of labels complicates the navigation for keyboard users, and fields with pre-filled information may go unnoticed, affecting the overall user experience. Users might mistake placeholders for automatically filled data, leading to confusion. Finally, users may encounter issues with manually deleting placeholder text, creating unnecessary burdens and increasing the interaction cost of form completion. It's crucial to prioritize clear labels and instructions to enhance user understanding and streamline the form-filling process.

Combining labels with placeholder text helps make forms better. Labels outside the fields show important information at all times, while placeholder text inside the fields should be extra hints or examples.

Even with labels, though, putting important instructions inside a field can still cause problems, even though they might be less bad. If some fields need extra information that's crucial for filling out the form correctly, it's best to put that text outside the field so people can always see it all the time.

Error Messages

We don't want users to read these texts, but we must create them with care because, in many cases, these messages will be the only guidance and explanations users receive. It's very unpleasant when the experience is interrupted due to an error. Therefore, we should explain simply and transparently that there is a problem and what it is (emphasizing that it's not the user's fault). Next, we need to explain how to resolve or work around the problem to accomplish the desired action initially. If the error is indeed the user's fault, such as entering an incorrect password, we should handle it lightly and always provide guidance toward a solution.

We proactively address errors: in other words, we make every effort to guide users so they avoid making mistakes and, thus, don't encounter error messages.

The following example serves as a great source of inspiration. In my view, the mascot shouldn't have tears in its eyes (as it may evoke disturbing feelings of guilt), but overall, the message is clear: Why can't you order food from this restaurant now? Because it's closed. What's next? It should reopen soon. The clever touch is the button at the bottom offering to notify the user as soon as the restaurant opens, allowing them to place an order. While it may not solve the problem immediately, it explains everything and provides a convenient option for users:

This restaurant is not accepting orders at the moment. It should re-open soon.

Gong

Chinese · Sushi · Asian

3.1K ratings

7 km Baner

Similar restaurants you might like

Ahling

Chinese, Seaf...

65-75 min

Mamagoto

Asian, Sushi, J...

55-65 min

One China by Malaka...

Malaka Spice

Chef's Special Meal Bowls Dimsum Menu

Notify me when it opens ▸

Our next example lacks creativity. The use of the expression "Oops" in error messages has become quite cliché. It's best to avoid it, especially since it doesn't effectively communicate the nature of the issue. In fact, it might even give the impression that the interface is mocking the user!

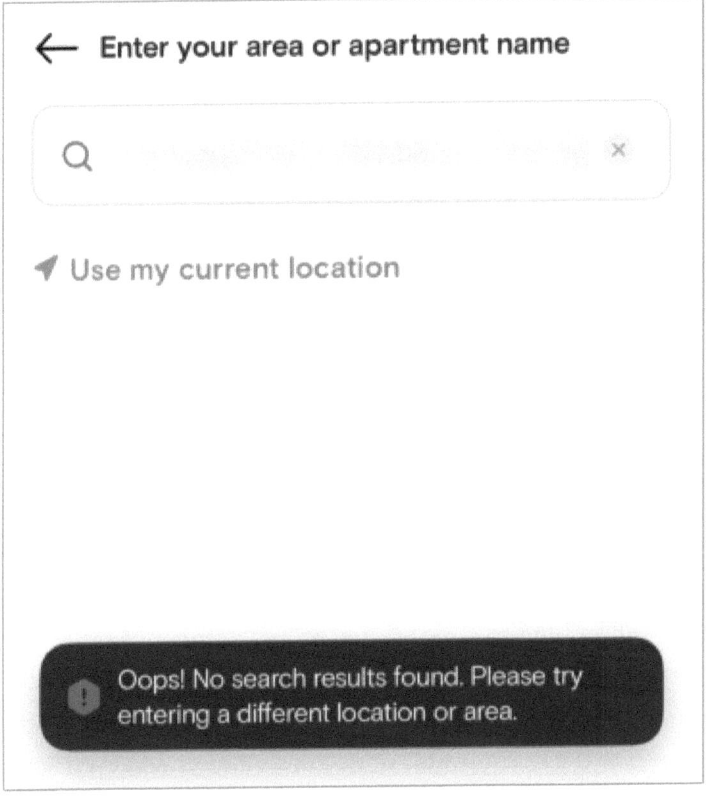

This example demonstrates what we shouldn't do: expose the internal error code to the user without offering a way out or providing guidance on how to solve the problem.

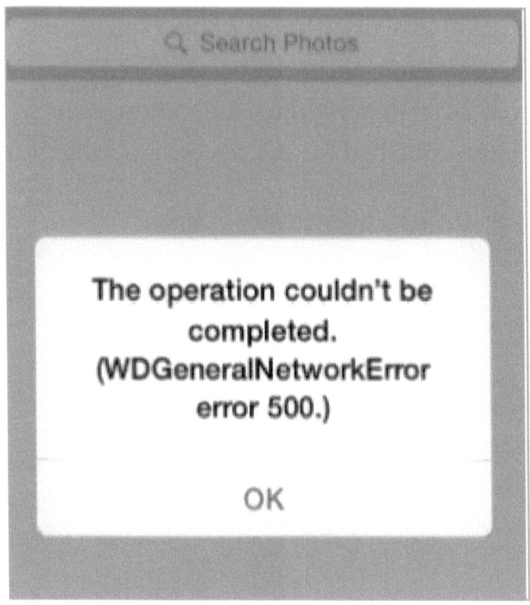

Confirmation Messages

These messages are essentially congratulations that we extend to users for successfully completing a task. Whether it's signing up, making a purchase, subscribing to a newsletter, or any number of other actions, users anticipate a confirmation. It's a friendly pat on the back that provides feedback, assures the user that everything went smoothly, guides them to the next possible or necessary action, and even has room for a bit of humor if the brand allows.

The key is to steer clear of clichéd and robotic phrases like "Registration completed successfully" (a redundancy that, although clear, could be improved) or "Purchase confirmed." If one of these is the headline, enhance the message with a description like "You did it! Wasn't that easy?" or something similar — let your creativity shine!

Here are some additional tips for writing effective confirmation messages in UX Writing:

Be Clear and Concise:

Clearly communicate the outcome of the user's action in a concise manner. Avoid unnecessary details.

Use Positive Language:

Frame the confirmation message in a positive light to reinforce a sense of accomplishment or success for the user.

Provide Next Steps:

Guide users on what to do next, whether it's completing a profile, exploring features, or taking another desired action.

Personalize Messages:

Whenever possible, personalize confirmation messages with the user's name or specific details related to their action.

Maintain Brand Voice:

Ensure that the tone and style of the confirmation message align with the overall brand voice and personality.

Avoid Jargon:

Steer clear of industry jargon or complex language. Make the message easily understandable for users of all levels.

Express Gratitude:

Thank users for their action, expressing appreciation for their engagement or decision.

Consider Humor (if appropriate):

If the brand allows, injecting a bit of humor can make the confirmation message memorable and engaging.

Use Visual Elements:

Consider incorporating relevant icons or visuals that complement the message and enhance user understanding.

Test and Iterate:

Continuously test confirmation messages to gauge user responses. Iterate based on user feedback and performance metrics.

Remember, the goal is to provide a positive and reassuring experience for users while effectively communicating the successful completion of an action.

This example is more complex because it involves several celebrated steps to complete the task:

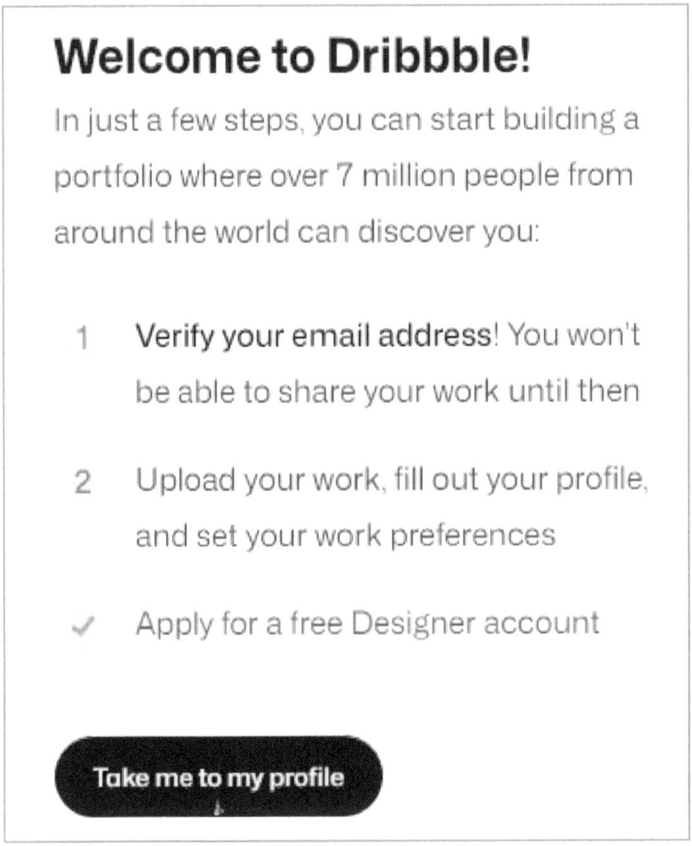

Welcome to Dribbble!

In just a few steps, you can start building a portfolio where over 7 million people from around the world can discover you:

1 **Verify your email address**! You won't be able to share your work until then

2 Upload your work, fill out your profile, and set your work preferences

✓ Apply for a free Designer account

Take me to my profile

The next one, however, incorporates almost all the previously mentioned recommendations: it is clear and concise, positive, provides next steps, uses the brand voice (the expression 'protected investment' reflects that), avoids jargon, celebrates, and includes a visual element (presumably the company's mascot):

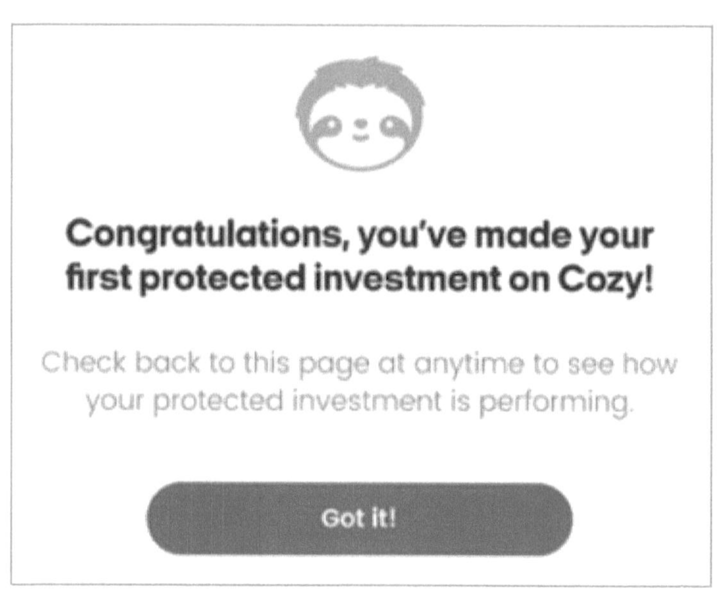

Empty States

When the user has not yet started their activities, the system may not have anything to display. However, an empty space is a waste of a resource that serves no purpose. Therefore, we need to leverage these empty spaces to encourage users, sometimes with a touch of humor, to engage with our website or app. Whether it's an empty shopping cart, the home page of your social media feed, or a backup folder without files, there's always an opportunity to influence user behavior positively.

In the following example, the empty state humorously portrays a deserted place without people (coworkers), still waiting for their invitation:

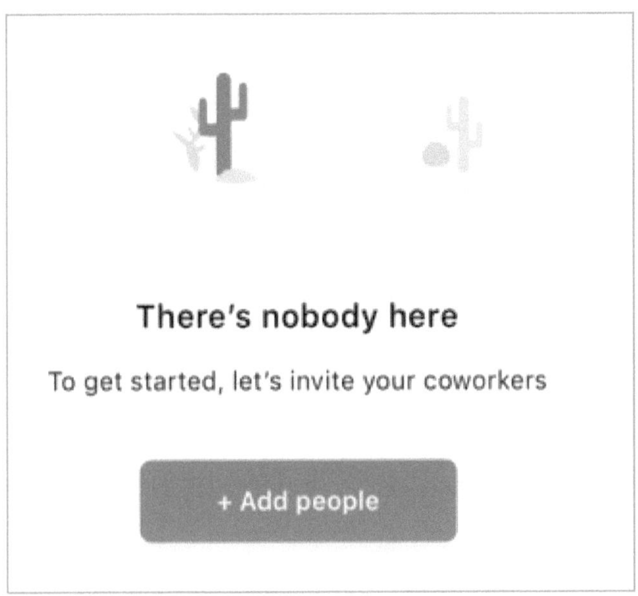

This one jokingly references the shopping cart, as if it could experience the emptiness:

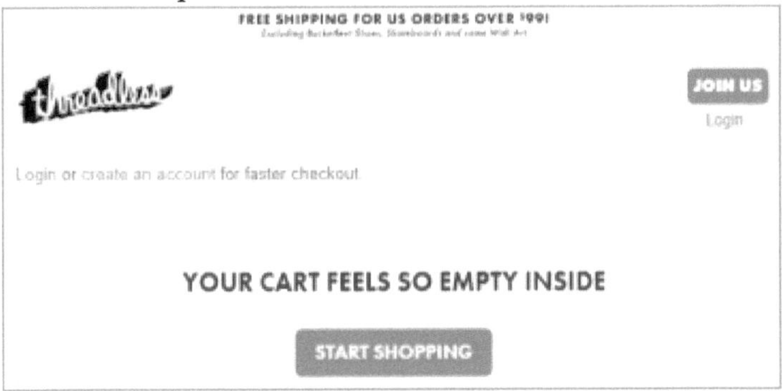

When dealing with an empty shopping cart, keep it user-friendly by adding a touch of humor or empathy in your messages. Let users know it's okay if their cart is empty, and suggest popular items or current deals to spark their interest. Use clear and friendly language to explain why the cart is empty and guide them toward the next steps, like exploring categories or taking advantage of special offers. By making the empty state engaging and helpful, you turn a blank space into an opportunity for users to discover more. The idea here is not to miss the chance to encourage potential business!

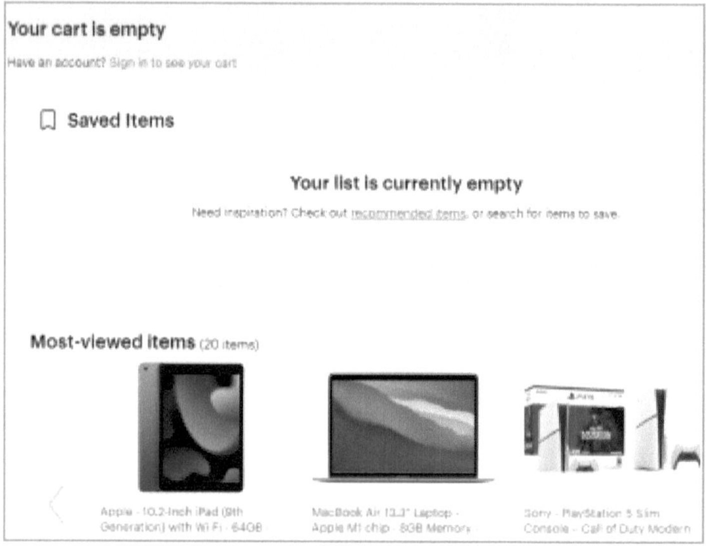

Controls

They are elements, sometimes just graphical, that indicate the state of an option. For example, on and off switches or even checkboxes for selecting an option.

They can mimic elements from the real, physical world or be graphical representations already established in users' mental models, such as arrow buttons that add or subtract.

In this example, we have a switch clearly selected as 'on' or checked:

Buttons (call-to-action or CTA)

Buttons serve to execute a specific action, functioning as invitations to action, literally calling the user for an action. It's crucial to consider the underlying action when choosing the appropriate verb for the button. Sometimes, a simple 'Continue' is sufficient when only one (or some) of several steps are completed. However, when the step is singular or final, opting for a more descriptive verb like 'Buy Now' or 'Subscribe to Newsletter' is advisable.

Considering the importance of conciseness, some professionals recommend keeping buttons within three words. Personally, I am not rigid about this and align with other experts who argue that more descriptive buttons can lead to higher conversions. You don't need to write a paragraph on a button, but adding a touch of flavor can make all the difference. For instance, an e-commerce platform offering fast delivery might use 'Buy Now and Receive Tomorrow' instead of just 'Buy Now,' or a registration process could be completed with a button saying 'Complete Registration to Start Enjoying.'

The first example focuses on specifying the target users, with three call-to-action buttons destined for three types of consumers: women, men, and children. In my opinion, a neutral (unisex) button is missing, especially to include non-binary and other gender minorities. However, these buttons are efficient because they will request only a specific type of product that best suits the needs of that particular user:

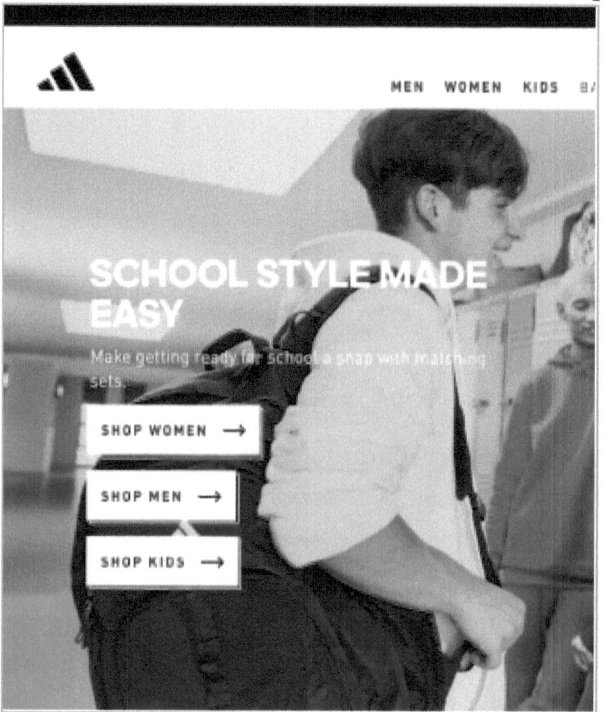

The next example is very specific about the kind of products the user will check if the button is clicked (desktop) or tapped (mobile). Instead of using only 'Explore,' which would rely on the implicit understanding of the subject of exploration, the button says upfront exactly what the user will explore:

Another descriptive and direct-to-the-point CTA is found in this button: it says "add payment details now." So, essentially, it starts by giving the user an order (add), specifying the action, then what (payment details), and finally, when (now). Very effective, but more than 3 words, illustrating my point that sometimes one or two more words are worthwhile because of increased clarity and/or persuasion.

Loom Starter comes with a **25 videos per user limit** as well as a **5 min recording limit**. Your Workspace will lose access to features like:

- **Unlimited videos** that let you store all the content you want
- **Unlimited recording time** that lets you capture and share longer recordings like presentation walkthroughs
- **Unlimited Transcription (beta)** that improves accessibility by letting viewers access an interactive transcript of your video's speech
- **Engagement Insights** that allow you to see how viewers have interacted with your video
- **Custom branding** that lets you add your company logo and color to your video

To continue with Loom Business, subscribe today!

Add Payment Details Now

The Loom Team

Error Pages (including 404)

Just like error messages, error pages are unwelcome not just for the user but also for the company, which doesn't want to lose visitors (possible leads). In the case of pages not found (404 error), it's the job of the UX writer to be creative and transparent with the user. First, explaining that there's been an error and what kind it is, and then providing various options for the user to try and capture their attention, keeping them within the brand's ecosystem and preventing frustration from leading them to simply leave the site.

In this first example, despite using the somewhat cliché "Oops," it promptly explains the problem in the title. It also acknowledges the user's emotions with the phrase "keep calm," followed by an instruction to refresh and try again (a somewhat vague instruction, but still better than providing no guidance at all).

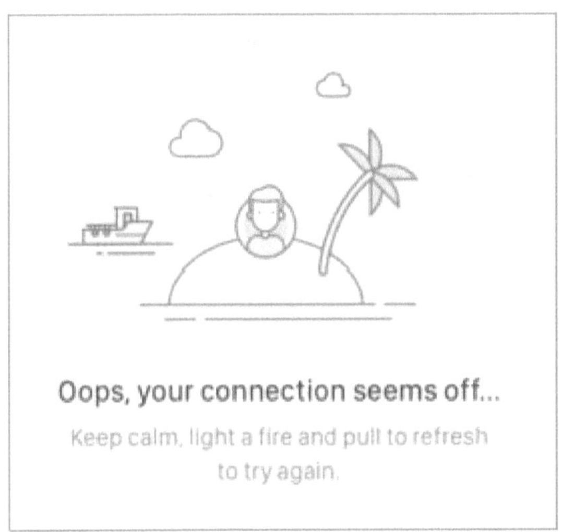

The next example displays the error code, which is useless for the user. However, it hits the mark when the text states that the user didn't do anything wrong; the error occurred due to the brand's infrastructure, not because of a user's mistake. This type of message absolves the user from any guilt. The button simply directs the user back to the home page, and like the previous example, it at least provides some direction.

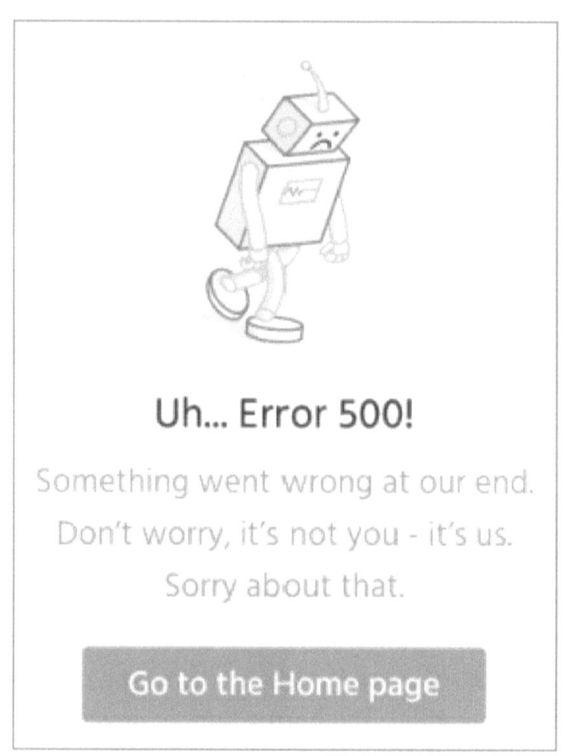

Our last error page/screen example provides a good amount of user-relevant content. Beginning playfully with "Houston, we have a problem," it reassures users that issues aren't their fault, identifies the problem and states that they are already taking care of it. Then, it suggests the user to return later, but also offers quick access to a chat and email for urgent matters.

Houston, we have a problem

Don't worry, it's not your fault. We are already looking into it.
Please, come back in a few hours.

Got an urgent request? Open chat

or send email to help@retargetapp.com

Search Results Pages

Often, we may not have precisely what the user is seeking, but that doesn't mean we can't provide them with a broad range of other relevant content. A search results page can not only present the direct results but also include suggestions for additional materials or areas within the website or application that might capture the user's interest.

To enhance user engagement, consider offering filters to refine the search, related topics, or even popular searches to guide them to more targeted information. Additionally, maintaining a clean and well-organized layout with clear headings and concise descriptions can significantly improve the user experience on search results pages.

In our example, we can see that even though the search did not return any items for the exact query 'slayer', the system proactively suggests other queries such as 'skater' and 'shaker,' attempting to provide a solution to the user in case of a typo. It then displays some popular products anyway, aiming to capture the user's interest.

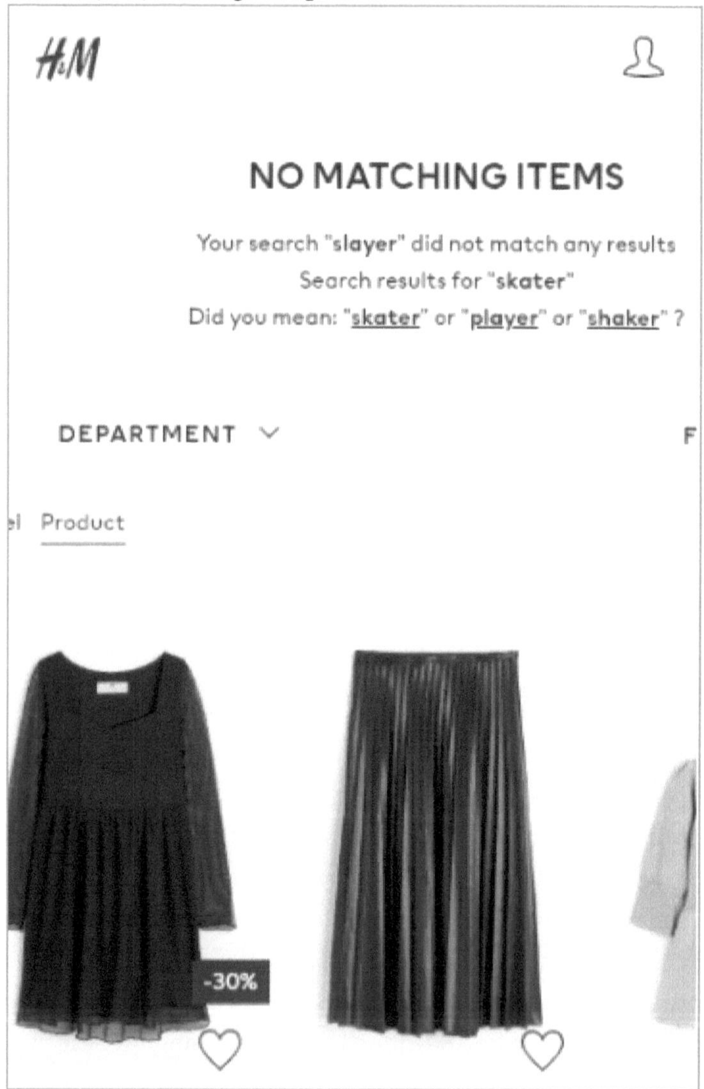

Transition Texts

These texts bear the responsibility of reassuring the user by explaining that something is happening, and they should simply wait. They can be straightforward and informative or infused with a touch of humor, reminiscent of the loading screens in Windows or certain games. Instead of a bland "Please wait..." message, they alternately present phrases with a sense of purpose, like "Wait while we customize your desktop" or "Building the universe of your game," followed by "Creating galaxies and planets," then "Crafting continents, mountains, and oceans," and so forth. Incorporating engaging and purposeful messages during waiting periods not only eases user anxiety but also adds an enjoyable element to the overall experience.

Additionally, when designing transition screens, it's crucial to consider the visual aspect alongside the textual content. Employing visually appealing graphics or animations that align with the theme of the task at hand can enhance the user's experience during the waiting period, transforming what might be perceived as a mere delay into an engaging and even delightful pause.

In this initial example, the animated loading status ring not only adds a visually dynamic element but also serves a functional purpose. It progressively fills, offering users a tangible representation of progress and a visual indicator of the time remaining for the completion of the process. Despite the ring's functional engagement, the accompanying text remains dry and lacks creative expression.

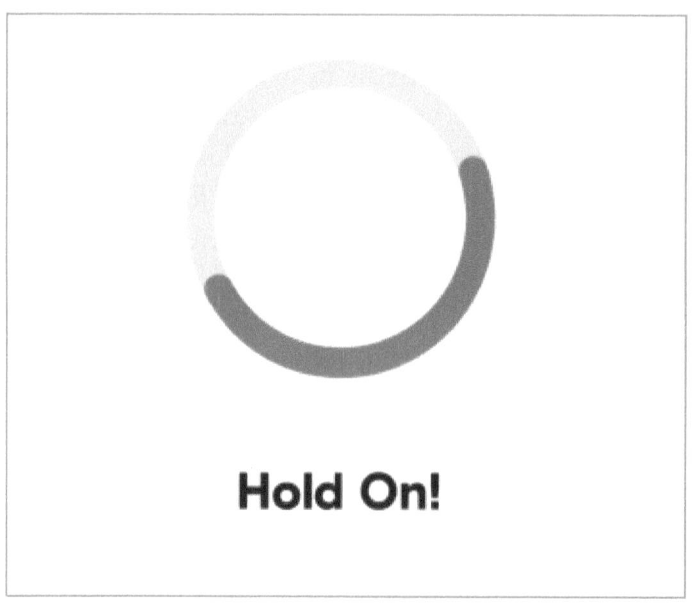

This example employs a technique known as a skeleton in User Interface design. It consists of light-gray placeholders that indicate in advance where elements will be positioned once the loading is complete. These placeholders give a preview of the locations for lines of text, images, new areas, etc.

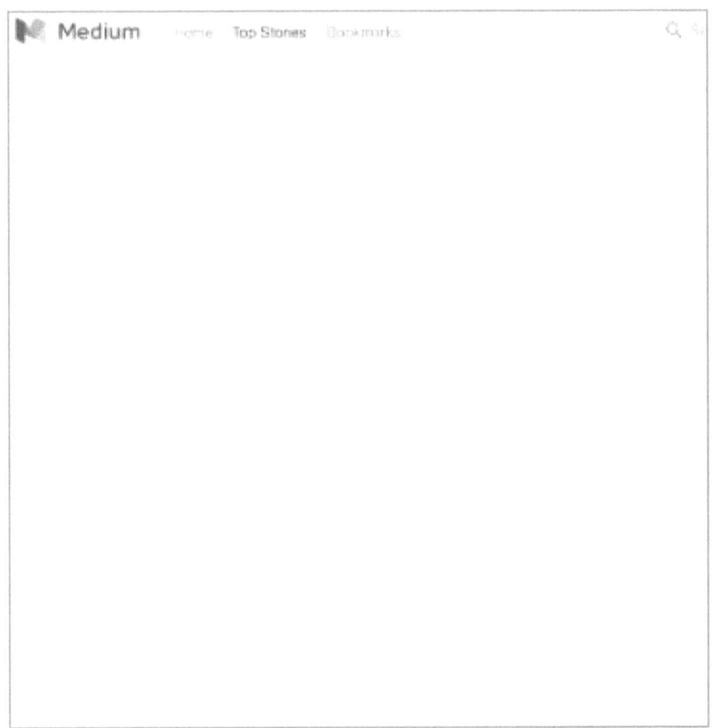

The ideal loading page is no loading page.

Providing interesting quotes for the sake of curiosity or a collection of progressive phrases that reports the current status of the loading, like "filling the tank," then "starting the engines," and "awaiting for the sign to go green," can be very helpful in alleviating the boredom of waiting and adding a touch of entertainment.

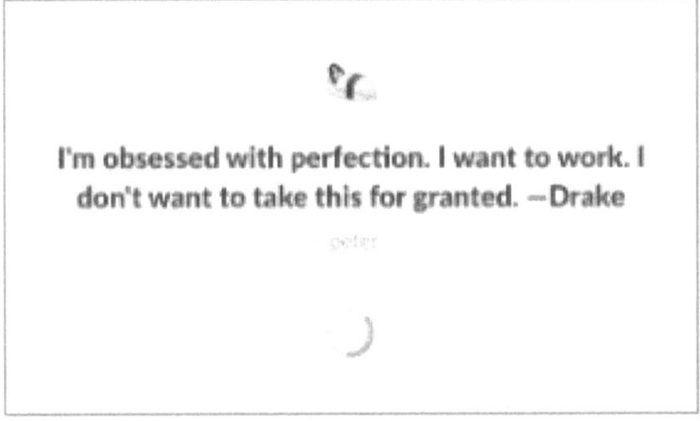

Google Chrome goes beyond expectations; in the absence of functioning internet, the presented screen allows the user to play a mini-game featuring a dinosaur running through the desert, needing to jump cacti to survive and accumulate points. While it doesn't solve any problem, it's surprising and indicates that some significant effort was put into creating an engaging screen.

While longer loading times may enhance user experience in certain cases by being entertaining, unintentional delays without proven benefits likely harm conversions and frustrate users.

Strategies like skeleton screens, animation, lazy loading, and humorous microcopy can mitigate frustration, but they only mask the underlying issue — waiting diminishes the user experience. The key is to prioritize optimizing your product for efficiency, speed, and quick loading to minimize waiting times.

How to write good links and CTA buttons

Back in the days of dial-up internet, when Queen Elizabeth and I used it to access the web, practically all the links on every site had the same text: "click here." Time passed, and new variations emerged, such as "read more," "see more," "continue reading," among many other uninformative variations.

To write the best text for links and buttons, they need to be specific, sincere, substantial, and succinct — according to a Nielsen Norman Group article.

Specific link texts tell the user what they will access or find after clicking or triggering such a link or button. This creates a more precise expectation about what is to come.

They need to be sincere because they make a promise: if you lead the user to believe, for example, that they will download the e-book by clicking the button, but instead, they are directed to a form before releasing the desired download, the user feels deceived. So use microcopy that is genuinely consistent with what will happen after activating the link or button. If your links are not sincere, the user's perception of your brand's trustworthiness will diminish.

When we say a link or button needs to be substantial, we are really talking about its composition: to be noticeable, it needs to have a different color from the rest of the text, perhaps a decoration like underline, be in bold or inside a button that is easy to spot when scanning the screen or page.

Finally, succinct is synonymous with concise: the fewer words (letters, actually) you use to clearly inform the user about the function of that link or button, the better. This way, the user saves time and enhances their experience, having their expectations met and knowing in advance what to expect.

And what about other types of text?

I like to think of UX Writing as a specialization within Web Writing, which itself is a subset of Copywriting. But it's important to mention that professionals from various fields can work as UX Writers, making the transition without necessarily having worked previously as Copywriters. UX Writing is much more about the intrinsic characteristics of design and its implications than it is related to persuasive writing or copywriting.

So, I believe that if the professional responsible for UX Writing has the appropriate background and sufficient knowledge, they can work supporting and collaborating on various types of text, including those on website pages, email campaigns, advertisements, brand communication through social media, and even blog posts.

Considering that the person experiencing the journey begins as a potential customer of the brand at every touchpoint, a UX Writer could also write beyond the digital realm, encompassing physical communication forms such as internal signage, banners, totems, posters, and certain types of flyers.

However, as most professionals seem to prefer, we can understand that UX Writing involves the research, planning, and crafting of interactive dialogues between users and digital products, such as websites, apps, software, chatbots, voice interfaces, automated teller machines, operational systems, CMSs, dashboards, CRMs, among others. By the way, the Brazilian Mergo User Experience School defines

UX Writing as "the creation of texts that help users achieve their goals, taking into account their mental models and motivations."

Use of emojis in UX Writing

In various cases, such as direct communication with users (via chat or email) or in other types of communication, such as ads and email sequences, UX Writers can use emojis. They serve as a complement to written language with letters. But one important detail: emojis should come after the sentence and punctuation, only one at a time, to be understood more clearly and by more people.

Of course, it's not always appropriate to use emojis; you need to analyze the brand voice and the tone of each message. So, UX Writers need to exercise discretion to decide when and if the use of emojis is valid.

The precursors of emojis, the emoticons, like :) or ;), are not as easy to understand and are also not correctly read by screen readers that visually impaired people often use. In other words, don't use them.

Inclusion and Diversity in UX Writing

For any business, the more paying customers, the better. There are some laws in the USA that are basically anti-discrimination laws. In the UX universe, and for us, UX Writers, thinking about everyone is an obligation.

So, how should we incorporate the principle of universal design into our work? Product designers often remember The Web Content Accessibility Guidelines (WCAG), that are like rules for making websites and digital stuff easy to use for everyone, including people with disabilities. These rules were made by different groups, like businesses, disability groups, and people from governments, to create a global standard. Even though following WCAG isn't a law, it's a widely accepted set of rules.

The goal of WCAG is to make websites, apps, and other digital things accessible to people with different disabilities, like those related to sight, thinking, learning, and physical abilities. It has many criteria that web designers, developers, and content creators can follow to remove barriers for people with disabilities when they use digital stuff.

But we know that design can go much further, including UX Writing. We have a duty to do the basics well, such as drafting satisfactory alternative text (alt tag describing images), using yellow emojis (their original color, which is easier to see and makes less distinction of people's skin color), adopting plain language, avoiding foreign terms and technical jargon, not using discriminatory terms (racist, homophobic, ableist, among others), encouraging non-violent communication, and trying to reduce the prevalence of the masculine in our writing.

In the English language, there are more possibilities to reduce male dominance. This includes opting for neutral options, which is less problematic than in Latin-derived languages such as Portuguese. In Portuguese, articles and pronouns often have a gender, and the default is usually male, accounting for about 98% of them. In English, this issue is less acute, as it mainly involves words like he/she and his/her. It's possible to use they/their in many cases, to write "Businessperson" instead of "Businessman" or "Businesswoman", "Humanity" instead of "Mankind," "Chairperson" instead of "Chairman." These may sound too progressive for some people, but it's a natural path for language because even if you are a very conservative person, you want leftists to buy from you, then you have to keep them satisfied with your brand. So it's vital not to mix your personal values with what's best for your business.

There is a widespread usage of 'Mx.' as an alternative to 'Mr.' or 'Ms.' However, it's unclear whether this title is correctly read by screen readers, potentially affecting individuals with visual impairments. Considering that there may be more blind or visually impaired users than non-binary users, it is advisable to test or seek feedback from your users on this matter before making a decision on its continued use. In job titles, you can use "Firefighter" instead of "Fireman" or "Flight attendant" instead of "Steward" or "Stewardess." When addressing a group, use "Everyone" or "All people" instead of "Guys". If you're talking about relationships, use "Partner" instead of "Boyfriend" or "Girlfriend."

When possible, try using both genders, for example: "This app is suitable for actors and actresses." It contradicts the idea of conciseness, a UX Writing maxim, but it speaks directly to more people.

We must remember that no matter the age, ethnicity, religion, skin color, sexual orientation, or gender a person identifies with, as UX Writers, we should not mention any of these conditions or peculiarities, only treat everyone with respect and as equals. People with disabilities are not "carriers of diseases" or "special." They are people, first and foremost, and only in a few moments will it be relevant to mention that they have a permanent or temporary disability (physical mobility impairment, visual impairment, hearing impairment, etc.). We should only mention or indicate a disability if it is related to something that is being addressed at that moment, such as when explaining an accessibility feature of a location, product, or content, for example.

Diversity and inclusion are extremely important and continually evolving topics. Talk to or interview people who are different from you, different from the majority of white middle-class people, try using your smartphone with only one hand or using only voice commands and a screen reader. We learn more every day about how we have prejudices, how we still do not respect some people, and how people suffer for not fitting within what is ignorantly considered "normal" by our Western culture.

The importance of FAQs

FAQ stands for Frequently Asked Questions, which are the most common queries that leads or customers may have. This database of questions and answers can be collaboratively created between UX Writers and professionals from other departments that also benefit from a well-structured FAQ, such as the Customer Experience area. This department often identifies new frequently asked questions, providing opportunities for cost reduction by offering easy-to-find answers to people without them needing to contact a company representative.

The reduction in service costs can be significant if the FAQ is properly maintained, regularly reviewed, and expanded based on feedback from those who interact with leads and customers. Sometimes, tool statistics may reveal terms searched in the FAQ that did not return relevant questions and answers, potentially leading to phone, chat, or email inquiries. Upon identifying such gaps, UX Writers can add these new questions and their answers to the FAQs.

It's also important to note that the FAQ aligns with Nielsen's tenth heuristic (help and documentation), making it largely the responsibility of UX Writers.

Complementary knowledge useful for the UX Writer

Just by analyzing the term 'UX writer' or 'Content Designer', we can uncover some clues about knowledge that can be useful for such professionals: 'Content', meaning mostly textual content — and 'Design', a term already consolidated and probably self-explanatory for someone reading this book. In academic circles, they often emphasize that design does not mean drawing but is more akin 'to compose' or 'to plan', maybe 'to sketch' or 'to blueprint.'

So, all techniques related to writing can be helpful: knowledge of spelling and grammar, understanding the concept of plain language, principles of good, clear and concise writing, the inverted pyramid, SEO best practices (search engine optimization), persuasive text techniques, marketing knowledge, taxonomy, information architecture, artificial intelligence prompt engineering, voice-controlled interfaces, chatbots, accessibility, and inclusion, among other subjects.

More related to design, we begin with the way of thinking (design thinking), go through methodologies and frameworks, the idea of continuous improvement, and reach principles related to perception, cognition, and aesthetics. Studying how the human brain perceives and interacts with interfaces can be very useful: from semiotics (in a blatant simplification, the science that studies signs, in the sense of images that we recognize as having a clear correlation with something in the real world), Gestalt (in another absurd simplification, the branch of psychology that studies perception) to Nielsen's heuristics. Jakob Nielsen is the longtime partner of Don Norman and co-founder of the globally renowned Nielsen Norman Group (https://www.nngroup.com/), which is highly respected by user experience professionals and designers. The institution practically defines the rules and serves as a reliable source for consultation and learning, as they are constantly updating their content and reviewing their recommendations.

An important read for anyone working with UX (user experience) is the book called 'Laws of UX Applied,' by Jon Yablonski, which contains a collection of psychology findings useful in crafting the user experience. You can explore these 'laws of psychology' in English on the author's official website: https://lawsofux.com/en/.

However, it's worth noting that every piece of knowledge can contribute to the work of a UX writer; after all, our primary subject of study is the human being, and diverse experiences can contribute in this regard: how much you know about human behavior, organization and documentation, frontend and backend programming, agile methodologies, among many other topics.

What is scannability?

In an ideal scenario, users of an application will pay attention to what they are reading, and this should include all titles, more descriptive texts (in paragraphs, also called support texts), lists, buttons, etc.

However, in the real world, the overwhelming majority of people (and the younger they are, the more natural this process becomes) generally **scan** the content they come across. This typically means reading most of the titles, glancing at some other words, and reading the buttons at the end of the content. That's why we need to work on what we've come to call 'scannability,' that is, how easy it is to quickly glance at a screen or page and understand the essentials without having to stop and read carefully.

At this point, important concepts come into play, such as the hierarchy of elements on a page, usually well-crafted in the layout done by SEO professionals. We should have titles that, on their own, can orient the reader, as well as buttons that are consistent with the titles (using the same verb, for example). Take a look at any good landing page and notice how it is structured.

How people read online

According to studies monitoring people's eye movements conducted by the Nielsen Norman Group, most individuals do not read texts in their entirety. They tend to scan, meaning they glance over to read some parts, key words, titles, bold highlights, the beginning of list items, etc. Study: https://is.gd/leituraonline.

A highly emphasized best practice is to alternate text with images in a zigzag pattern, where texts and images are diagonally arranged. Another interesting finding pertains to highlighted quotes or ads that interrupt the textual flow of an article, for instance: if a person has started reading calmly and attentively, when they encounter one of these elements, they change their behavior and start scanning the text, as if they have lost interest or patience to consume the information in its entirety.

During the process, which we refer to as "scanning," people may skip sections, go back to previously skipped items, reread something highlighted, and so forth. Despite the zigzag tendency, scanning can be quite chaotic and vary depending on the reading objective. People tend to read if they have motivation and if the content is important to them. When they are seeking more specific information on a particular topic, scanning occurs by searching for occurrences of words related to the subject of interest.

These studies have established visual hierarchies of titles with different weights, the use of subtitles or lead, placing essential information at the beginning (inverted pyramid style), the use of lists, bold text, and simple language to engage (and include) as many people as possible.

The path followed by individuals paying more attention has been nicknamed the "lawn-mower", as reading begins at the top left, moves in a line to the right, then descends and moves in a line to the left, restarting the cycle. However, the most common pattern detected was the F-shaped scanning format.

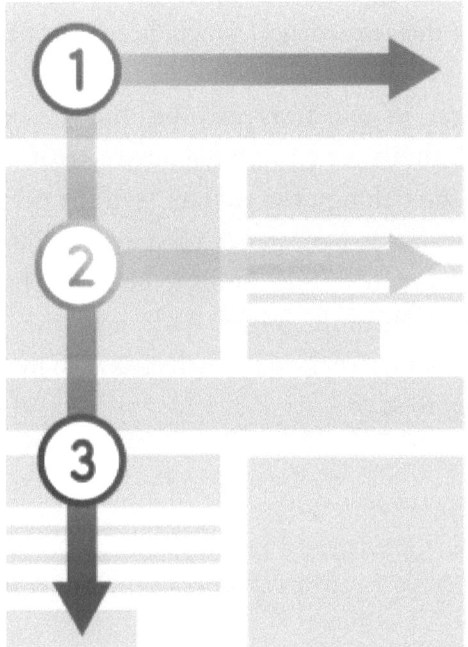

As if people paid a bit more attention to the title and the first lines (or subtitle) and immediately started scrolling for other elements that catch their eye. One of the most evident findings of the study is that people do this because they don't want to waste time or make an effort when consuming online content.

On landing pages, we should place the main content in the first two paragraphs, use titles and subtitles, start paragraphs with the two most important words about the topic, group related content, use bold for emphasis (in moderation), employ descriptive links and buttons (instead of generic "click here," for example), utilize bullet or number lists, and cut anything unnecessary.

On a mobile app screen, it's crucial to seek the following combination: an explanatory title and a button with a compatible and logical verb, with supporting text serving only to provide more context for those willing to read or seeking a more comprehensive explanation.

When this is possible, we reduce the cognitive load of the flow for the person, streamlining their experience, which, in turn, is perceived more positively.

As concise and clear as our texts may be, fun and easy to understand, we should always aim to communicate what is most important, considering three things: the context — if the person has reached that point, they already have some expectation or intention; the title, which can use more than three words to describe what came before that screen and where it might lead; and the button (call-to-action), which should have the same verb present in the title or be highly complementary to it.

UX Research in UX Writing

Some UX professionals go so far as to say that without research, there is no User Experience work. This is because all types of research support the decisions made, the paths chosen, and those ignored. Like in any field, research is divided into quantitative and qualitative, with the most common types (among UX Writers) being:

Desk research: Also known as secondary research, this method involves seeking and gathering information from pre-existing documents to extract knowledge about something specific. Information collected from research conducted for other purposes, internal company records, periodicals, books, etc. Care must be taken regarding the credibility of sources.

Text interpretation test: One of the simplest, it involves handing your text to someone (preferably a representative user of the product) and asking a few questions aimed at confirming whether your text made sense and was properly understood.

Interviews: Can be conducted with users or other individuals directly involved with the product. When conducted with users, it is ideal to transcribe or record to assist in the development of controlled vocabulary. Interviews provide qualitative information about users and key stakeholders.

Highlighter test: In this test, participants receive two highlighter pens, one red/pink and the other green/yellow. The first color is used to mark passages considered difficult to understand or incomprehensible.

The second color is for passages that are more friendly or enjoyable to read.

Card sorting: In it, several words (which can refer to products, services, or anything else) are placed on cards (physical or digital) and then grouped according to each person's logic participating in the test. It can have predefined categories, such as market areas or types of products, or allow people to create their own categories. With this method, we are investigating the taxonomy that makes the most sense, not for us, but specifically for our audience. This method is useful for defining sitemaps and information architecture.

Questionnaires: offers a structured approach to understand user preferences and behaviors. They provide both quantitative data and qualitative insights, helping researchers gain a valuable understanding of how users interact with content. The calculation of sampling, reliability, and margin of error can be a bit complicated, but to assist in this task, there are free online tools, such as this one: https://is.gd/comentto.

A/B Testing: When testing two options with a similar user base to discover which option is more efficient.

Prototype testing: After the UX designer completes the first navigable prototype, it can be tested with users to analyze if the product is understandable, if the texts are having the expected effects, and (of course) if the visual design is intuitive enough.

Cloze Test: it is done using a text, removing keywords, and asking people to fill in the empty spaces with their own words or with predefined words.

Analytical data: Not only access to analytics data but also more advanced data can be obtained, such as heatmaps, recorded navigation sessions, and sophisticated recordings of user gaze (eye tracking).

More research and testing frameworks from the UX Writers' world

The following content is a suggested approach based on practical experience, established best practices, and shared insights. As always, it's ideal to test what works for you in your context.

Any design or user experience professional needs a clear understanding of the problems they aim to solve, the pains they intend to address, and the specific objectives their work aims to achieve. It all starts with a question, for example:

- What do I want to know about my users, and why do I want to know this?

- Which problem of my company should be prioritized, and how can design contribute?

From there, we have some categories:

- What do people do?
- What problems do they face?
- What do they need?
- What do they want?
- Can they use a particular product?
- Who are they?

The first framework that can be used is called the **CSD matrix**, which stands for Certainties, aSsumptions, and Doubts. In this matrix, we create three columns with the aforementioned categories and fill them with sticky notes (like post-its) in each column. This allows us to have a broader view of what we already know, what we assume to know — and it is crucial to be rigorous in classification to avoid considering our biases, that is, biased and unverified ideas, as certainties — and also what we are clear about not knowing yet.

Another widely used framework is the **empathy map**, a tool designed to better understand the user and their needs, enabling researchers to put themselves in the users' shoes. It consists of six main elements representing the problems, desires, demands, ideas, and feelings of people in relation to the company.

Let's take a closer look at each of these elements:

- **"See":** refers to observable aspects such as the user's physical environment, usage contexts, visible behaviors, and interactions.

- **"Hear":** involves active listening, understanding expressed opinions, needs, and desires.

- **"Think and feel":** encompasses the customer's internal thoughts and feelings, their motivations, expectations, fears, and aspirations.

- **"Say and do":** reflects actions and behaviors, including the distinction between what they say and how they behave in certain situations.

- **"Pains":** represent the problems, frustrations, and obstacles faced by users.

- **"Gains":** represent the desired benefits and outcomes, that is, what they hope to achieve.

By filling in these sections of the empathy map, we can obtain valuable insights into the needs and expectations of users or customers, which will help guide the development of products, services, and even sales strategies.

Empathy map example:

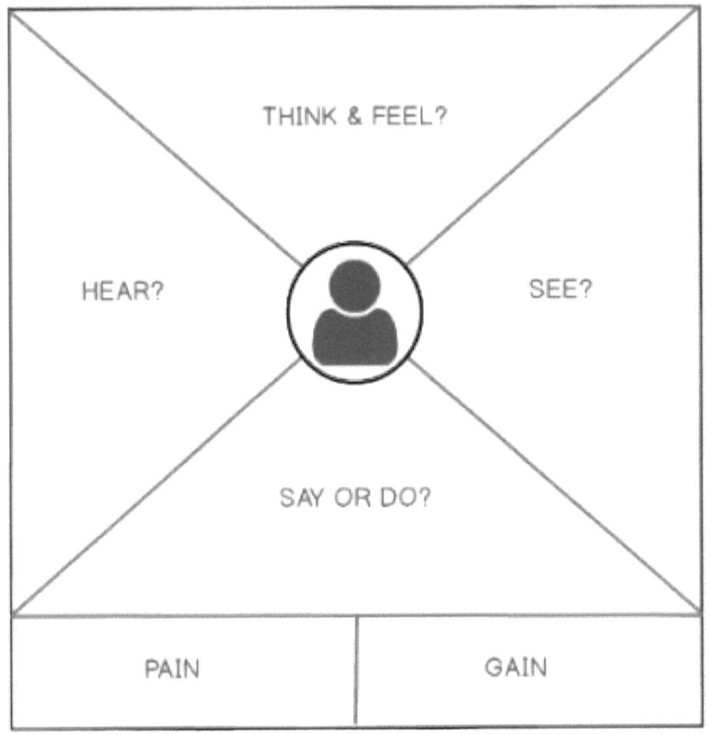

Another type of research, a bit more complex, is **field study**, in which UX professionals analyze users in their environments, in their day-to-day lives. It involves studying, listening, observing, and interacting with people in moments when their pains and needs emerge. With the collected data, we can understand what can be addressed with solutions within our reach, and then plan and create precise solutions that will assist people in their specific contexts.

As the obvious needs to be spoken (or written), it's also worth including the importance of **interviews** in this discussion. They can be conducted with users (who may be leads or customers, if they have not yet used a product) and also with stakeholders. Interviews can be structured (with a predefined list of questions), semi-structured (with a flexible list of questions, allowing additional questions based on responses), or unstructured (without predefined questions). It's also important to emphasize that these interviews should be individual, meaning they are different from focus groups, where multiple people are consulted and converse with the researcher. Some tips for conducting effective interviews include:

- Prepare follow-up questions, which in some cases may become relevant depending on the progress of the interview and the answers provided.

- Avoid questions that can be answered with a simple 'yes' or 'no' — it's worth considering the construction of each question so that the person can elaborate on the subject.

- Ask one question at a time, avoiding the concatenation of multiple questions in sequence, as often happens in press conferences with journalists' questions.

- Be careful with how you formulate questions or react to answers to avoid biasing, reinforcing, or disapproving of what the interviewee is saying.

A method that demands a bit more engagement from the analyzed individual is the **continuous usage diary**, a methodology that allows understanding the usage habits of a product or service over time. It is similar to a field study, but with the difference that the researcher is not present during data collection.

In this approach, it is the user who records their observations and notes in a diary, following a predefined script. It can be useful for mapping routines and providing insights into the lives of the people under investigation, serving as input for the creation and conceptualization of new products or services.

The continuous usage diary allows capturing usage data over different periods, in a natural context and without the direct interference of a researcher or the influence of being under observation. It can be applied, for example, to understand the needs and expectations of users before the launch of a product or to map user opinions about an already launched product, in contrast to their expectations.

A significant advantage of this method is providing information over time and in real usage contexts, with the recording of aspects related to the learning curve, registration, onboarding, and changes in perception over time.

Continuing along the lines of popular methods, we must remember **benchmarking**. In summary, it involves researching and gathering as much information as possible about how other companies are operating and what they are offering to their users. Here, it's worth taking screenshots of competitors' app screens, requesting quotes, pre-registering, using websites like Mobbin, seeking the help of friends and family who are customers of companies whose apps we don't have access to, and so on.

If you want to explore other interesting frameworks, look up for:

- H.E.A.R.T.;
- MoSCoW;
- RACI Matrix;
- JTBD (Jobs To Be Done);
- UX Honeycomb;
- BASIC UX;
- B = MAP;
- Hooked Model;
- Sacrificial Concepts;
- 5W2H;
- How Might We;
- The 6 Hats;
- User Need Statement (NN/Group), etc.

Controversy surrounding NPS (Net Promoter Score)

Although the Net Promoter Score (NPS) is easy to measure, produces a traceable number, and seems legitimate, various research studies have shown that it does not help companies grow and does not reflect customer loyalty.

The NPS calculation is based on a simple question asked to respondents: "On a scale of zero to ten, how likely are you to recommend company X to a friend or colleague?" The results are grouped into three categories: promoters (scores 9 and 10), neutrals (scores 7 and 8), and detractors (scores from 0 to 6). The NPS is then calculated by subtracting the percentage of detractors from the percentage of promoters.

However, even Fred Reichheld, the creator of the NPS calculation, acknowledged that it has issues. Small changes in responses can lead to significant changes in the final result, which doesn't make mathematical sense. Additionally, the NPS point scale is not clear, and respondents may struggle to distinguish differences between scores. Responses, collected outside the context of product or service use, may also not necessarily reflect actual recommendation or loyalty behavior.

Another common criticism is that the NPS focuses on predictions of future behavior rather than analyzing customers' past behavior. Questions about future recommendations are not reliable indicators of loyalty, current satisfaction, and do not provide an adequate understanding of customer behavior.

A 2007 study concluded that "the intention to recommend alone is not sufficient as a single predictor of future customer loyalty behaviors. The use of multiple indicators, rather than a single predictive model, significantly performs the role of predicting recommendations and customer retention better," available at https://is.gd/estudonps.

Despite much controversy, the Net Promoter Score continues to be widely used by companies as a primary indicator of customer success or satisfaction, and it is likely that this stance will not change in the near future. So you need to learn the essentials about NPS because it remains very much alive in the corporate world.

From design to text: what are usability heuristics?

In the 1990s, the Nielsen Norman Group defined a set of best practices for good design called heuristics. Heuristics are "procedures and standards used in research through the quantification of proximity to a certain goal," according to Michaelis On-line. However, in the case of User Experience, they are principles we should follow to achieve the best usability.

Let's explore each one and establish the connection between design and the text of the User Experience:

1. Visibility of system status:

"The design should keep users informed about what is happening through appropriate feedback for a reasonable amount of time." In the text, the UX Writer is always informing the user about what is happening and what will happen.

2. Compatibility between the system and the real world:

"The design should speak the user's language. Prefer words, phrases, and concepts familiar to the user over internal jargon. Follow real-world conventions, making information appear in a natural and logical order." Although this principle was originally intended for design, it fits perfectly into the text of the User Experience. It's the language that should sound natural, human, dialogical, never robotic or impersonal.

3. User control and freedom:

"Users often make mistakes unintentionally. They need to be able to clearly identify an 'emergency exit' without going through a lengthy process." In UX Writing, we try to provide action options and solutions for all possible problems.

4. Consistency and standardization:

"Users should not have to wonder if different words, situations, or actions have the same meaning. Follow market and product conventions." Another case of a heuristic that directly applies to textual content. Headings should "talk" to buttons, for example.

5. Error prevention:

"Good error messages are important, but the best designs carefully prevent problems from occurring in the first place. Eliminate error-prone conditions or check them and present users with a confirmation option before committing to the action." UX Writing has the same purpose of preventing problems but achieves it through clarity in communication and instruction.

6. Recognition rather than recall:

"Reduce the user's memory load by making elements, actions, and options visible. The user should not have to remember information from any other part of the interface. Information necessary for design (e.g., text field labels or menu items) should be visible or easily retrievable when needed." This principle justifies what we mentioned earlier about creating forms using only placeholders — everything should be natural and familiar to the user, never difficult or confusing.

7. Efficiency and flexibility of use:

"Shortcuts — hidden from novice users — can speed up interaction for experienced users so that the design can cater to both user profiles. Allow users to customize frequent actions." In an app, we can offer different options to the user in the settings. On a website, we can display only part of the information and a tooltip, which, one click or tap away, will provide more content on the subject.

8. Aesthetic and minimalist design:

"Interfaces should not contain irrelevant or rarely needed information. Every extra piece of information in an interface competes with relevant information units, decreasing their relative visibility." That's why we always seek conciseness, in addition to the fact that mobile devices usually have less space to display texts. Some professionals recommend that microtexts have up to forty characters and be distributed over up to four lines.

9. Help users recognize, diagnose, and recover from errors:

"Error messages should be expressed in simple language (without error codes), precisely indicating the problem and constructively suggesting a solution." Another case of a heuristic that directly addresses the text as a protagonist.

10. Help and documentation:

"It is best if the system does not need additional explanations. However, documentation may be necessary to help users understand how to complete their tasks." One type of content that I haven't mentioned yet but can be part of the UX Writing universe is Frequently Asked Questions (FAQs), a good example for this heuristic.

The 8 golden rules of Schneiderman

Ben Shneiderman is an American computer scientist and university professor whose work is recognized and respected by interaction designers as much as the works of Jakob Nielsen and Don Norman. Let's explore Shneiderman's 8 golden rules of interface design, presented in his book "Designing the User Interface: Strategies for Effective Human-Computer Interaction," and relate them to textual content.

1. Strive for consistency

Use familiar icons, colors, menu hierarchy, button text (calls-to-action), and similar user flows when designing situations and action flows. Standardizing how information is conveyed ensures that users can apply their knowledge from one interface to another without having to learn new representations for the same actions. Consistency helps users become familiar with the digital environment of the product, facilitating the achievement of their goals.

2. Enable frequent users to use shortcuts

Such as keyboard shortcuts in desktop software, allowing them to perform tasks more quickly and easily as they become more experienced. In texts, we can think of abbreviations, such as using the full name (United Nations) once and then only the acronym (UN), or names of months, among other words that do not hinder understanding.

3. Offer informative feedback

Ensure users know where they are and what is happening all the time. Each action should have an appropriate and understandable response in a reasonable time. For example, when filling out a multi-page questionnaire, it is helpful to indicate which step the user is on. Avoid error messages with complicated codes (like the famous Windows blue screen) and provide clear, easy-to-understand messages.

4. Design dialogs to yield closure

Provide clear conclusions for users, informing them of the results of their actions. This can be done through thank-you messages, purchase receipts, or other types of feedback indicating the completion of a task or stage. This ensures that users feel satisfied, relieved, and prepared for the next action.

5. Provide simple error handling

Give simple explanations of errors and step-by-step instructions for dealing with them. When errors occur, offer clear feedback and guidance on how to quickly and uncomplicatedly resolve the issue. For example, highlight text fields that users have forgotten in an online form, with a message explaining the fact.

6. Permit easy reversal of actions

Allow users to undo what they have done, whether after a single action, data entry, or a complete sequence of actions. This reduces anxiety because knowing that errors can be undone encourages users to explore unknown options. CTRL + Z to undo something when using the Windows desktop system is a classic example.

7. Support internal locus of control

Make users feel in control of actions in a system. Designing the system to behave according to users' expectations helps gain their trust. Therefore, before significant actions, request confirmation using, for example, a modal (content that appears prominently like a pop-up, while the area around it darkens).

8. Reduce short-term memory load

Make interfaces as simple as possible by using an appropriate hierarchy of information and favoring recognition over recall. Recognizing is easier than remembering because it involves perceiving clues (we will talk more about clues, nudges, or nudges ahead) that help access memory and bring relevant information to the surface. For example, it is recommended to use multiple-choice questions instead of open-ended short-answer questions.

Many of these 8 golden rules are **similar** to Nielsen's 10 heuristics. They are principles specifically designed for human-computer interaction design, but they are not exactly heuristics — which are generic rules discovered through trial and error, observation, and common sense. Going a step further, we can even say that these heuristics are recommendations based on facts discovered through research and analysis with scientific rigor. Nielsen's 10 heuristics form a set of usability principles that help identify issues and provide solutions to enhance the user's interaction with a system or interface.

Nudges and dark patterns

'Nudge' can be interpreted as a 'push,' a type of encouragement that occurs in the way the text is presented to the user or how a question is constructed. It is part of choice architecture, a branch of behavioral economics. Despite sounding like a great ally for persuasion, conversion, and the success of a business, it is essential to be very careful about how we shape the choices of our leads and customers. The term gained popularity with the book of the same name, released in 2008, written by Richard Thaler and Cass Sunstein.

In Brazil, it's worth noting that the complete title of the translated book became 'Nudge: The Push for the Right Choice,' in the sense that nerds associate with Spider-Man's uncle: that great powers bring great responsibilities.

In other words, once you have knowledge that can influence people's decisions as a soft push, it is crucial to consider the ethics behind this incentive, potential consequences, and the limits that should be respected not to nullify people's right to choose.

Influencing them to make choices aligned with our interests, even if such choices are not necessarily beneficial for them or are even harmful, is what we call in the design field a 'dark pattern.' These are deceptive experiences that take advantage of people's habits when using websites and apps to induce them to do something they did not intend.

These actions have the sole purpose of benefiting the company. They can include strategies such as disguising ads as content, using manipulative language, hiding cancellation options, or making access to important information difficult.

These tactics aim to direct the behavior of users subconsciously and often deceptively. With this in mind, it is important to recognize if we are producing something that falls into this category and avoid the use of dark patterns in the design of digital products, as they completely compromise transparency, ruin trust in the brand, and greatly harm the user experience.

What are the deliverables?

Among the key materials produced by UX Writers is the **writing guide**, which contains the brand's voice and tone. This documentation, mentioned earlier, flirts or intersects with branding strategies.

The writing guide may include a glossary of terms used internally in the company and also a controlled vocabulary dictionary, which requires a semantic immersion in the target audience's universe to identify the words most commonly used by these individuals.

It is essential to make it clear that telemarketing is not UX Writing, although it is advisable for the call center and sales team to always follow the writing guide to speak and write according to the brand's voice. On the other hand, chatbots are generally included in the tasks of UX Writers because they are literally dialogues between products and users.

In daily operations, it is recommended that UX Writers learn to use graphic development and prototyping software, such as Figma and Adobe XD. While these professionals will not create layouts or work on the visual design of things, they can edit the text directly in the design and get a good idea of how it will look after development, ensuring that it fits well in designated spaces, avoiding widows (single words on the last line of a paragraph), and ensuring correct information hierarchy, among other considerations.

It is also suggested to use a task manager, such as Trello, to record the refinement work of the texts, as it is the kind of work that can consume a lot of time but generate little concrete material immediately, even though subtle changes can have significant impacts on results, a fact that will only be measured at a later time when testing or product usage begins.

That takes us to another important topic: documentation.

The importance of documentation

Something seldom discussed, to our surprise, is the documentation of the UX Writing discipline. Keeping a record containing a summary of the reasons, objectives, and progress of the work can be essential for future references, for the preparation of reports, or for measuring the overall work. Additionally, it creates a history with the evolution of the product or feature being worked on.

There is no widely discussed and validated standard within the community, but some basic elements can be part of the documentation. One suggestion would be to have three types of documentation:

1. One for priority and larger projects.
2. One for common day-to-day demands.
3. A simplified one, intended for small tasks (the famous 'quick jobs' when someone calls you in a hurry to help decide on the text for a single button or screen, to make a paragraph more concise, find a good synonym for a term, etc.).

Speaking of more generic elements to include in the documentation, we can suggest the following:

Project Name: Every task needs to be named, even if it's just a numbering to identify and differentiate it from other demands.

UX Writer: Your name, of course.

Requester or Responsible Person: Who requested or is responsible for the product or feature you will be working on.

Stakeholders: Other people involved in the approval and development of the demand.

Status: Update this as the work progresses.

Objectives: The project's goals and the objectives it aims to achieve.

Context: Describe the status quo, i.e., how the situation is before the delivery of the product or feature.

What We Know: Summarize all relevant information you already have, whether based on simple desk research or obtained through more in-depth studies.

Problems to Be Solved: or pains that we aim to improve or address.

Appropriate Tone of Voice: Specify the most suitable tone of voice for the situation.

Related Journey Moments: If you have access to the user journey mapping, list moments related to the product or feature in question.

Description: What is the reasoning behind your work, i.e., what strategies you are implementing and how you are thinking of successfully completing the work.

Before and After: The last but not least important item to document; it can be an image of the before (or perhaps just a note that there is no available screenshot), and alongside it, another one showing how it looked after your intervention.

When should Product Designers include UX Writers in the beginning of the process?

In a simple answer: always. At every stage of the design process, the perspective of Content/UX Writing can help, complement, be decisive, or provide clarification. And it doesn't matter if the process is based on the double diamond or something similar and more customized: the contributions are diverse and often save a lot of time and/or effort at any stage.

It's common for teams, especially agile squads, to underestimate the potential contributions of individuals with sharper skills related to text, instructions in interfaces, brand tone and voice, audience vocabulary, among other details that UX Writers meticulously master more than user experience professionals who are not content specialists.

Sometimes, these content-focused professionals may have less background in digital interface design, aesthetics, cognitive psychology related to symbol recognition, or the effect of colors on perception. These are interesting and valuable topics for any UX professional, but sometimes the insertion or omission of a verb on a screen, for example, can make the user behave in completely different ways — thus being a decisive factor in the success criterion for a particular workflow being worked on.

In practice, with design teams having a much smaller number of UX Writers, a commonly used strategy is to train the team on creating protocopy, i.e., low-fidelity microcopy, UX Writing in a draft version. So, instead of noting 'Here goes an instruction about the current step' or placing a generic 'Lorem ipsum,' Product Designers (or UX/UI Designers) can reflect a bit and sketch an initial version of the textual content that will be present in their prototypes. Often, this reflection is already enough to provoke changes in the project, such as reducing screens in the flow, solving a difficulty with a small additional informative text on an existing screen, or even the more accurate conclusion about which components a particular screen needs.

Nevertheless, these initial versions should be reviewed and refined by UX Writers to ensure:

- The choice of words that are easy to understand for the audience of that digital product;

- Consistency with the rest of the product and with the brand voice;

- Titles and buttons (or CTAs, calls-to-action) that are compatible with each other so that even if the user ignores the supporting text, they can still locate themselves and have a reasonable understanding of what they are doing or what is happening at that moment;

- The correct use of the English language, according to the possible peculiarities of the brand voice;

- Clarity, conciseness, and, when appropriate, that the text feels conversational.

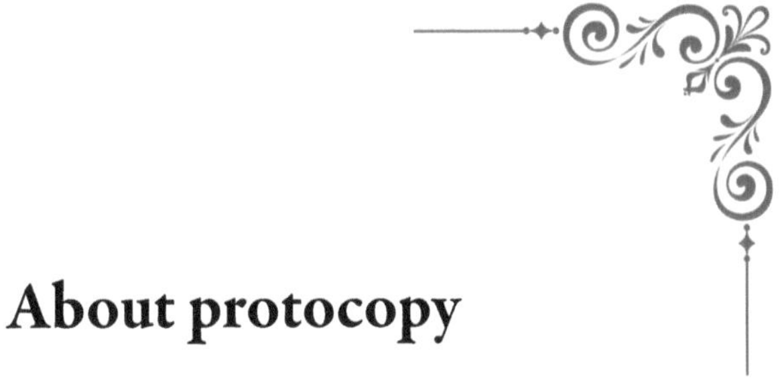

About protocopy

As mentioned earlier, it is possible to train such professionals (Product Designers or UX/UI Designers) to produce protocopies instead of using the infamous placeholder texts like 'Lorem ipsum' or literal instructions of what textual content should be in that location. However, even if they cannot learn or dedicate time to refine the textual elements of their flows, these individuals must provide broad context about the solution they are working on so that UX Writers can understand the needs and specificities of the screens where they will enhance the textual content.

As it is common for UX Writers to work in multiple squads (or products) simultaneously, it is necessary to prioritize some and rely on the support of Product Designers for the rest: they should have well-organized documentation on the discovery, an explanation of the logic of the proposed solution, the goals of the prototype, and, in more specific cases, describe who the users are and with which words or terms they are accustomed.

For example: in a team with only one UX Writer, they align with their leadership that they will focus on the mobile application that customers use, but other squads in the company work on desktop products used by customer service professionals. As dedicated Product Designers in those squads, these professionals have the opportunity (or duty) to know the users of the solution they continuously work on, including their own repertoire of specific terms used by the users of that product (creating a glossary).

In these cases, for the textual content to be satisfactory, it is essential for UX Writers to receive all this information that they could not obtain because their focus was entirely dedicated to another squad, its ceremonies, its solutions, and users.

What to avoid writing in digital product interfaces

We know that texts or microtexts created for user interfaces (UIs) should be clear, concise, and useful. People need them to achieve their goals (and your company's goals as well). So, let's discuss 14 things you can avoid to ensure better quality in your deliveries:

1. 'Oops' and other cliché words are, for various reasons, personally recommended to be avoided by me, Atila Velo. This includes the possibility of being misread (as in "ohps") and because they do not distinguish your brand from the crowd. Additionally, some words don't mean anything.
2. Details about errors and system failures should also be avoided since it won't make a difference for users to know the error code (only developers can do something about it). If we provide too many details, users will need to think more before arriving at a possible solution. Our content should always suggest an action for the user, even if it's as simple as 'try again later.'
3. Always evaluate your texts by asking yourself, 'Does my user need to know this?' in the quest for more conciseness, trying to stay below 40 characters per line, and no longer than 4 lines.
4. Define in advance and maintain consistency if you are going to write microtexts in the first person, imperative, or infinitive (examples: 'I want to subscribe,' 'Subscribe,' 'Subscriptions').

Using 'I want to create an account' and then a link to 'Your account' will be inconsistent and potentially confusing, even ambiguous.

5. Avoid writing numbers in full, for two reasons: it is simpler and quicker to read a number in digits, and it will likely take up less space (e.g., 22 instead of twenty-two).
6. When addressing the user, remember that they are unique and irreplaceable. Address them in the singular form (avoid plural references like leads or clients).
7. Avoid excessive use of uppercase letters, even if your brand's voice permits it. Use it sparingly to prevent users from feeling like you're shouting at them and to maintain a hierarchy of information based on semantic structure, not just typography space.
8. Moderate the use of exclamation points too! Otherwise, it may give the impression that you are in a hurry! Or worse: shouting at the user! Perhaps with disproportionate enthusiasm?!
9. Trim the fat: instead of asking, 'Would you like to create a new document?' consider using 'Create new document.'
10. Sayings and proverbs: even if you grew up hearing everyone around you repeat a saying or proverb, remember that they can be very regional, distorted over time, or too abstract for some people, compromising the clarity of your content.
11. Avoid confirmation buttons in modals or any screen space with a question in the title and options like 'Yes,' 'No,' 'Cancel,' or 'OK' – to avoid ambiguity, repeat the action verb on the button, such as 'Delete' or 'Send.'
12. Error messages that are too vague or don't suggest a solution for the user, like displaying 'Fill in all mandatory fields' during registration – instead, specify which mandatory field was not filled in or which password security requirement was not met

by the entered password.

13. Never blame the user: remember that if they can't do something right in your product, it's your team's fault for not anticipating the needs of the product's users. Never write things like 'You caused an error in our server,' 'You selected the wrong option,' or 'I don't want to be smart and receive the newsletter' (a dark pattern case).
14. Even proficient writers can stumble into common pitfalls. Differentiating 'its' and 'it's,' 'there,' 'their,' and 'they're,' and 'your' versus 'you're' are crucial. Misplaced modifiers, when descriptive words are not close enough to the words they are meant to modify, leading to uncertainty. Confusing 'fewer' (countable items) with 'less' (uncountable). Awareness of these mistakes is vital for improving writing quality.

Remember that after 'etc.' that ends the sentence, there is no need for an additional period. There are many good and easy-to-understand websites that can help you write correctly, answer your questions, and provide free text verification services, such as in the text editing software itself (Google Docs, Microsoft Word, OpenOffice or LibreOffice Writer, MacOS Writer, OnlyOffice, etc.) or other more specialized services, such as the very useful Hemingway App (https://hemingwayapp.com/).

The double diamond and UX Writing

The double diamond is a popular design approach originating from Design Thinking, aiming to solve challenging problems through a structured and iterative process. The methodology consists of four phases: **discovery**, **definition**, **development**, and **delivery**. The consolidation of this method occurred after its creation by the UK Design Council, gaining popularity from 2009 with the generic mission of improving lives and things through design.

In the **discovery** phase, the goal is to deeply understand the problem and identify the needs and goals of the end-users. It's a moment of research, analysis, and collection of relevant information.

In the **definition** phase, the information gathered earlier is compiled and analyzed, establishing a focus for solving the problem. This is the time to gain clarity about the challenge to be addressed, whether related to an interface flow or not (just as UX Writing is not just a small piece of text, UX Design is not just a screen — both disciplines, and design in general, aim to come up with solutions for people and business problems).

In the **development** phase, numerous solution ideas emerge, grounded in the data collected and consolidated in previous phases. It's the time to explore different approaches and, when applicable, prototype possible solutions to the identified problem.

Finally, in the **delivery** phase, solutions are tested (often directly with end-users), then refined (including checking with software engineers, front-end and back-end developers, the feasibility of the planned solutions) and implemented by the product, design, and technology trio. It's the time to validate the generated ideas and put them into practice.

The double diamond is crucial for the digital product design process because it guides designers in solving complex problems in a structured way. It is a clear working model (or framework) that helps maintain focus on the needs of end-users and **iterate** continuously until solutions that truly work to address the initially mapped pains with stakeholders, Product Managers, and user feedback, either directly or via CX (customer experience).

The work of UX Writing can also adopt the double diamond for execution because UX Writing plays a fundamental role in each of the phases of this process: it involves creating texts and content that enhance the user experience in digital products, providing clear and concise information, appropriate guidance, and feedback.

For example, in the **discovery** phase, UX Writers can work on analyzing all existing content, identifying gaps, and understanding the communication needs of end-users.

In the **definition** phase, UX Writers can contribute to defining the brand's voice and tone, communication principles, and language to be used in the product, according to the context of the solution and respecting all documentation about voice and tone.

Arriving at the **development** phase, UX Writers get hands-on and actually engage in creating texts for prototypes and developing microcopy, such as buttons, error messages, and usage instructions. When there is no visual interface, the role of UX Writing can involve adapting the language of documents or artifacts generated by the squad, among other cases.

Finally, in the **delivery** phase, UX Writers participate in validating language and content, ensuring that information is understood by end-users and that communication is effective.

How to make the job migration

Even though it's not in as high demand as it was a few years ago, it's an area that tends to survive well against the advances of generative artificial intelligence. The more mature design teams become, the more in-demand the role of UX Writing will be, including the support of top business leadership. It is also important to share that UX Writing has been increasingly referred to as Content Design, despite there being some significant differences in scopes. So, UX Writers end up being called Content Designers, but not necessarily do they possess as broad expertise as one needs to be a Content Designer. We will address the topic further down the line.

To transition into the UX field, a writer should aim to create a portfolio focused on UX, even if it includes fictional pieces. This could be the result of UX Writing Challenges or any interface where you present a 'before and after,' providing context for the improvements you would make to that digital product and the reasons behind those changes. Include a detailed explanation of the reasoning and motivations that underpin these alterations and enhancements.

How does the advancement of artificial intelligence impact the work of UX Writers?

Is the future of work in User Experience at risk?

Since the rise of ChatGPT, Midjourney, and DALL-E, there has been much debate about the future of work in general. Similar to the Luddites in the 18th century who, feeling replaced by machines, revolted and destroyed equipment, it seems that soon many tasks performed by humans will be done with better quality by artificial intelligence. The obsolescence of human labor in many activities is inevitable and will likely cause much confusion and require adaptation by individuals, businesses, and governments.

As of November 2024, we are still in a discovery phase, witnessing the rapid rise of this theme (hyped) in all industries, services, and other spheres. The future, in precise and detailed terms, is impossible to predict, but what is widely discussed among digital product design professionals is that a distinctly human ability highly sought in this field will extend the lifespan of our professions: empathy. Others also mention soft skills or behavioral abilities, as well as effective people management.

It can be envisioned that, as long as the economy relies on consumption, people will need jobs and, to be productive, will continue to need tools. Thus, there is a chain effect ensuring the need for the existence of various professions, albeit increasingly less manual and repetitive, less artisanal and organic, less original and innovative. Given that the economy continues to depend on human actions and people continue to consume, there will be a need to keep producing, innovating, improving, and reinventing various aspects of our lives.

The rise of AI has made mastering prompt writing essential for writing professionals. As AI systems become more sophisticated, crafting the right prompts has emerged as a crucial skill, guiding AI to generate effective, contextually appropriate content. Professional prompt writing appears to be the natural successor to traditional writing roles, as it combines elements of copywriting, UX writing, and technical writing into a single, impactful skill. In a world where AI is central to content creation, prompt writing is shaping the future of the writing profession.

People at the center, not robots.

Therefore, design focused on the user experience will remain a discipline of people studying people to enable them, through products (whose formats are unpredictable going forward), to achieve their goals, perform tasks, and take the necessary actions for their survival, well-being, and the continuity of the species on the planet. Artificial intelligence arrives as a powerful ally for most professionals, with the potential to replace or drive the evolution of less complex professions, yet still capable of existing as something that enhances human capability rather than replacing it.

If (or when) artificial intelligence surpasses human writing abilities, fully grasping nuances, emotions, and mental models, a human touch will still be essential. There will always be a need for someone to feed the AI with relevant data and craft the precise prompts to steer it effectively.

Everything indicates that the ongoing changes could greatly benefit our world. They may help accelerate the preservation of nature, reduce income inequality, eradicate hunger with increased rural productivity, among many other possibilities for advancements that, if dependent solely on human intelligence, would take much longer.

So, embrace the moment, seeing new technologies as allies — day-to-day partners that have emerged to maximize our intellectual capacity.

The main differences between UX Writing and Content Design

There was a time when the two terms seemed to be synonymous, but as the community debated the subject, each became more well-defined. Translating, UX Writing would be writing for the user experience, while Content Design would be something like Content Project Management.

From what I gathered from the latest discussions I attended or read, UX Writing would be the discipline of Content Designers, much like UX Design is the discipline of Product Designers. UX Writing is more connected to the creation of microtexts (microcopy), while Content Design encompasses thinking about various formats, including traditional design principles to enrich content and help the user achieve their goals.

Despite this, in a study conducted by Aaron Raizen, available at https://is.gd/uxwvscd, it was identified that job positions advertised as Content Designer often diverge significantly from the expected scope. In Brazil, the term has been gaining more strength and followers — in a path that seems irreversible.

To make it easier for them to find you, for example, on LinkedIn, it's better to describe yourself as UX Writer | Content Designer — just a tip. In summary, the Content Designer remains a UX Writer, but has a slightly broader view than just working with text. This person is also a designer: a Content Designer.

A bit about ContentOps, DesignOps, and Design System

These three names might be very familiar to you, or perhaps you've never heard of them. But none of them is a bogeyman, so let's demystify each one, briefly.

ContentOps can be a role, a group, or a way of thinking, with a focus on the management, production, standardization, quality assurance, and consistency of content, usually textual, for a brand. When a role or group, individuals have the responsibility to establish UX Writing standards and disseminate the tone and voice guidelines throughout the company. When it's a way of thinking, it happens after the company has reached a minimum level of UX maturity, especially in the textual aspect.

DesignOps can also be a role, a group, or a way of thinking, but its focus is on defining and optimizing design team processes, integrating and fostering good relationships among team members, standardizing documentation, defining quality, managing tools, supporting the recruitment process, onboarding, and offboarding, promoting knowledge sharing and learning within the design team, leading ceremonies like retrospectives and health checks, and evangelizing the entire company about the value and potential of design. In essence, it's about people, processes, and tools.

Design System, on the other hand, is a set of custom and shared libraries used by the entire design and technology team, containing components tailored to the brand's needs and following branding rules, ensuring maximum accessibility and facilitating the construction of new wireframes by providing all the necessary elements for creation already prepared, configured, and tested. Everything added to a design system comes with descriptive documentation and all the information the interface builder needs, as well as everything developers need to deliver with quality and agility.

And what about the **Content System**? It has started gaining popularity and is essentially a set of textual components fully integrated into the design system. Unlike the tone and voice guide, which contains style guidelines and definitions, the Content System includes reusable elements for everyone in the product + design + technology triad. These are standardized words, phrases, or texts for specific recurring uses, duly tested and approved by UX Writers. It is usually within the Design System, as a part of it.

Recommended readings

- Strategic Writing for UX - **Torrey Podmajersky**
- Microcopy: The Complete Guide - **Tenneret Yifrah**
- Laws of UX - **Jon Yablonski**
- Don't Make Me Think - **Steve Krug**
- The Design Of Everyday Things - **Don Norman**
- Writing Is Designing: Words and the User Experience - **Andy Welfle**
- Articulating Design Decisions - **Tom Greever**
- Content Strategy for the Web - **Melissa Rach**
- Conversational Design - **Erika Hall**
- Building a StoryBrand - **David Miller**
- Everybody Writes - **Ann Handley**
- Mapping Experiences - **Jim Kalbach**
- The Non-Designer's Design Book - **Robin Williams**

- Nonviolent Communication - **Marshall Rosenberg**
- Content Design - **Sarah Richards**
- User-Centered Design - **Travis Lowdermilk**
- Waking Up - **Sam Harris**
- Hooked - **Nir Eyal**
- Neuro Design - **Darren Bridger**
- Science and Sanity - **Alfred Korzybski**
- UX Design - **Will Grant**
- AI: First New UI Paradigm in 60 Years - **NN/Group** (https://www.nngroup.com/articles/ai-paradigm/)

www.ingramcontent.com/pod-product-compliance
Ingram Content Group UK Ltd.
Pitfield, Milton Keynes, MK11 3LW, UK
UKHW042017190726
13854UKWH00005B/2334